IN SEARCH
OF SILENCE

IN SEARCH
OF SILENCE

POORNA BELL

**SIMON &
SCHUSTER**

London · New York · Sydney · Toronto · New Delhi

A CBS COMPANY

First published in Great Britain by Simon & Schuster UK Ltd, 2019
A CBS COMPANY

Copyright © Poorna Bell, 2019

The right of Poorna Bell to be identified as the author
of this work has been asserted in accordance with the
Copyright, Designs and Patents Act, 1988.

1 3 5 7 9 10 8 6 4 2

Simon & Schuster UK Ltd
1st Floor
222 Gray's Inn Road
London WC1X 8HB

www.simonandschuster.co.uk
www.simonandschuster.com.au
www.simonandschuster.co.in

Simon & Schuster Australia, Sydney
Simon & Schuster India, New Delhi

The author and publishers have made all reasonable efforts
to contact copyright-holders for permission, and apologise
for any omissions or errors in the form of credits given.
Corrections may be made to future printings.

A CIP catalogue record for this book
is available from the British Library

Hardback ISBN: 978-1-4711-6921-2
eBook ISBN: 978-1-4711-6922-9

Typeset in Bembo by M Rules
Printed and bound by CPI Group (UK) Ltd, Croydon, CR0 4YY

MIX
Paper from
responsible sources
FSC
www.fsc.org   FSC® C020471

For Mum and Dad, because you are the first two people I ever loved.

For my sister, Priya, because you are the third. Because this is a song of everything I am, and who I became, and it began with you.

It seems to me that, if we love, we grieve. That's the deal. That's the pact. Grief and love are forever intertwined. Grief is the terrible reminder of the depths of our love and, like love, grief is non-negotiable. There is a vastness to grief that overwhelms our minuscule selves.

We are tiny, trembling clusters of atoms subsumed within grief's awesome presence. It occupies the core of our being and extends through our fingers to the limits of the universe.

Within that whirling gyre, all manner of madnesses exist; ghosts and spirits and dream visitations, and everything else that we, in our anguish, will into existence. These are precious gifts that are as valid and as real as we need them to be. They are the spirit guides that lead us out of the darkness.

– Nick Cave

Contents

PROLOGUE

'Auntie Poo,' my four-year-old niece, Leela, says plaintively.

'Mmm?' I reply, looking up from my book. We are in my sister's warm living room, cuddled up on the sofa in a mound of cushions and blankets. A phrenology bust regards us sternly.

'What is "married"?' Except she isn't old enough to curl the 'r's, so it sounds like 'mawwied'. She looks at me. Her eyes are huge like mine, and they have been like that since she was a baby.

Where my eyes are green with an iris of flame, hers are the inkiest black. Though she is barely over a thousand days old, she is looking at me with those dark, solemn eyes like an ancient creature, as old as meteors passing through space.

I swivel a desperate eyeball at the stairs, but my sister and brother-in-law are lost in a black cosmos of exhaustion: the sleep of grateful parents.

Here goes nothing . . .

'Well, you know Mama and Daddy?' She nods. Her curly hair flops over her eyes.

'So, Mama and Daddy are a couple. They're married. They love each other.'

'Okay,' she says. 'And what about Ajja and Dodda?' Ajja and Dodda are the names for Grandpa and Grandma, aka Ashok and Jaya, my parents.

'Ajja and Dodda are also married. They are also a couple and they love each other.'

I see her brain whirring, and, finally, she nods. I realise she will never see me with her uncle Rob, who passed away three years ago. My sister Priya has taught Leela about him, and I have given her books about all the things he loved – from the stars to the trees – with his name inscribed in the cover, but she will never remember him holding her.

A fine dust of sadness settles onto my shoulders.

Then she asks: 'Will I get married?'

I look at her unlined face. I breathe in the magic and potential of her. Imagine: a creature that has not been told what it should be yet.

I feel a pang; I never want her to know sadness or disappointment. I want her universe to stay safe and small. I want her to be this perfect, sweet little thing that hasn't been ground down by the world. But I know better, and I know that eventually these things come for us all, and all we can do is love the people in our lives well.

Sunlight lances through the room of our little kingdom and I bend down and place my hands on either side of her face. A pair of older green eyes look into the pair of beautiful black ones belonging to the smallest member of our family.

Through my hands, a silent wish of love, protection and kindness *and a promise to protect her from anything that might hurt her. But, for now, a gift of words.*

'Leela,' I say, 'you can get married, but you don't have to get married. You can fall in love, but you don't have to fall in love. You can live in a boat, a tent, a house. Wear socks as gloves and gloves as socks. You can be a princess, a ninja, a pirate, a painter – you can be everything and anything. But, above all, be what you want to be.'

She nods but doesn't say anything, because this is not the Auntie Poo she knows – the one who is silly, who flings her about in wrestling matches, tickles her while in character as a giant squid and yanks her socks off to do sock puppet theatre.

I don't know if she understands any of what I am saying, but I know that every time the world comes along and lays its expectations at her door, when it whispers dark thoughts and says, 'I will tell you the kind of thing you are . . .', I will hold her hand and look the world in the face and say, 'No. Let us tell you the kind of thing YOU are.'

1

EAT, PRAY, F**K YOU

It is spring in London, a late afternoon in April tugging at the threads of dusk. As the light softens to amber, a breeze slips through the streets to quieten fat buds of cherry blossom grown hot and flustered in the warmth.

The city has that pleasant hum of people migrating to parks for after-work picnics clutching bottles of prosecco, boxes of cocktail sausages. They line the pavements of pubs, sprawl across beer terraces like plants thirsty for sun.

It is a city that begins to flicker with mad hope, evident in the tiniest of ways – from commuters wiggling toes into flip-flops to people packing away their winter coats.

My friend Aman and I have forsaken outdoor activities for a hipster Indian restaurant, and our contrariness is rewarded with seats on narrow wooden planks better suited to teenage buttocks. Like a pair of ancient rotisserie chickens, we rotate different pieces of our anatomy at regular intervals to ease the discomfort.

'Small plates Indian food,' I say, peering at the menu. 'When did this become a thing?'

Apart from the benches that would not sustain even a third of the average Indian aunt's butt, there are kitsch little lanterns and pretty printed tablecloths. Not forgetting the real reason our mothers would slipper us over the head for entering such an establishment: minuscule pots of curry at an eye-watering £20 each.

As we swizzle our coriander-and-mango vodka cocktails like the middle-class wankers we are, I start to tell Aman about an idea I have.

'So I've decided to quit my job,' I tell him. Aman works in corporate law, loves the money, the members' clubs, and this is tantamount to me telling him I'm going to forsake my possessions, wear a sack and beat myself with twigs.

His eyes bug out and he stops mid-sip. A piece of coriander is peeping out at the corner of his mouth like a green hand waving hello.

'And *why*', he says, 'would you want to do that? Your job is amazing, and you get to do lots of really cool shit.'

'Yes,' I concede, 'my job is amazing, but that's not the point.'

'Then what is?' he asks.

'You know,' I mumble, 'being happy. Having some time out.'

Aman is happily married to a doctor and he and his wife have a two-year-old girl. He's a cool guy, a loyal friend, but when it comes to family and career, he has the same mindset as a 1970s Indian pharmacist. He always goes for the most conservative, traditional option. When his daughter grows up, if she decides to do what I'm doing, he'd probably have an aneurysm.

Looking at his disdainful expression and hearing the words come out of my mouth, I start to waver. This seemed like such a great idea, with some extremely valid reasons behind it. But explaining it is like trying to separate the yolk from the white; one wrong move and it will come out in a mess.

'Okay,' he says, digging a fork into a teeny pot of quail biriyani. 'And what are you going to do with this "time out"?'

I take a deep breath. 'Well, I wanted to travel. Spend some time away from London, you know, see the world a bit. I've never done the travelling thing. And I could maybe write about it.'

I can see the emotions flicker on Aman's face. *She's making a mistake. I should be more supportive. Jesus, there's a reason our mothers never cooked with quail . . .*

'Right,' he says slowly, 'and where would you travel?'

'Um, well, I'm going to try Italy, then India, possibly Thailand, and then I'm going to stay in New Zealand for a bit.'

'Hang on,' he says, while spooning more food on his plate. 'Are you basically going to do *Eat, Pr . . .*'

I point my fork at him.

'If the next two words out of your mouth are "pray"

and "love", I am going to stick this so far up where the sun doesn't shine, even your doctor wife isn't going to be able to remove it with forceps.'

He holds his hands up in defeat. 'Okay,' he says, 'why don't you start from the beginning?'

I put my fork down and begin.

~

The mistake I make, when trying to talk about why I've made this decision, is that I am trying to use Aman's vocabulary. It is too narrow; his rules are too precise.

He sees only with his eyes, he feels only with his heart; no wonder my words are muddling. I am trying to articulate something so magnificently complex in his rudimentary language.

But that's okay, because he doesn't have to approve of what I am doing – in this he is merely a witness. While I would like his validation, and that of all my loved ones, I don't need it.

Two years ago, before I sat in this restaurant to tell the first of many friends why I was leaving a very good job as executive editor at *HuffPost*, a huge and terrible thing happened.

On 28 May 2015, at 1am, while staying at my parents' house in Kent, I received a phone call from my mother-in-law, Prue. I was married to her eldest son Rob and he had temporarily moved back to his home city of Auckland while we worked through a separation.

It was a call that would change all of our lives, the ground zero beginning with Prue, my father-in-law David and myself, and radiated out in a ripple.

It engulfed anyone who had ever known Rob, anyone who had kissed him, held his hand in friendship, laughed alongside him, rubbed his shaved head, bopped around to music, come to his house to eat at his table, danced with our dog Daisy, shared a cigarette with him.

Through Prue's tears, her voice originating from a point so painful, the raw place where people have lost their children, she told me that Rob was dead. He had been found in the woods by the police. He had taken his own life.

Even though we knew Rob had been missing for twelve hours prior to this, that he had said his final goodbyes to all of us, that he had a previous history of suicide attempts, I heard my voice say with broken hope, 'Are you sure it isn't a mistake?', because this couldn't happen to us. This type of horror belonged to someone else, to some other family.

Because even though we had been separated for three months because I had reached breaking point dealing with Rob's ongoing problems with addiction and depression, we were in love with each other when he closed his eyes for the last time.

Love was meant to conquer all; it was meant to make Rob well again so that one day we might get back together. Love was not supposed to stand aside like a coward as the person I loved most desperately stepped through a doorway I couldn't enter. Love was not allowed to let him die.

But he did die. And so the vast being I thought was love was changed altogether, and it could never again be the hopeful, hyperbolic, naïve, cosmos-altering thing I had dreamed of since I was a kid. I always knew, once found, that it was a rare and precious thing, but now it was something far deeper, complicated and sad, but also more honest.

No matter how many times people tell me it wasn't my fault, no matter how many times I tell *myself* it wasn't my fault, there is always a part of me that says, 'But if you were in love with him, how could you leave him? If he was in love with you, how could he leave you?'

And, in order to answer that honestly, we must put aside our childlike notions of love. We must extricate ourselves from the Hollywood notion that love is simple and that the right words at the right time can provide salvation.

We must allow the dark ink of reality to write our past, present and future, in words that are honest and, ultimately, hopeful.

2

THE UNDERRATED BURROWS
OF MORAY EELS

Six and a half years before the phone call that blew apart my world, there was a phone call of a different kind. This was the phone call that introduced Rob into my life.

We'd been set up on a blind date by our mutual friend Tania, and it's testament to Rob's charm that it didn't creep me out that he a) Googled a picture of me before we met and b) told me he'd done so during our first date.

My first impression, when we met at a Brixton sushi restaurant, was that he was a man unlike any other I had met. His broad shoulders and rolling swagger were deceptive: beneath the shaved head and the sharp jawline was a massive nerd who loved baby owls and nature and gardening.

Instead of scaring me off, however, his contradictions only drew me towards him.

In this he was the flame and I the moth (although he would have almost certainly said it was the other way round). He was a science journalist who actually had money and owned his own house (most journalists are bum broke and grift for freebies – I have cadged everything from holidays to a mattress in my time).

He was from New Zealand – a place I didn't know much about beyond its 'more sheep than people' reputation. His photo, sent ahead of our date, showed him next to his dog, Daisy. In dating circles, men post pictures of themselves with their dogs because they've heard it's appealing to women. Except Daisy, while beautiful and the colour of sandstone, looked like she would chew your arm off as a snack.

It wasn't just that he was razor-sharp in his wit on email; he seemed like a straightforward, relaxed guy who listened to The Specials.

I didn't have to check planetary alignments about the right moment to text him in case he got spooked off. I could be honest and soft with my heart because he was the same.

What started haltingly on my side – I couldn't quite believe that there was this clever, beautiful man who was interested in me and he wasn't a weirdo – soon snowballed into a full-blown love affair. As each week passed, another room expanded inside of me until he occupied every inch.

'Why do you want to marry him?' my father asked, six months later, when I had asked him and my mother on a seemingly innocent country walk, only to ambush them with our intention to get married. Mum – normally so talkative her stories often had to be culled halfway with our exasperated groans – was strangely silent, intently studying a centipede on the ground.

Rob had met them in their Kent home a handful of times, appearing nervous, sweaty and eager to impress. But they didn't really know him. However, considering how my love life had been a sad, saggy state of affairs in my twenties, I thought they would've been happy that I had finally found someone I wanted to settle down with.

Lord knows I'd heard enough eye-rolling comments from people over the years ranging from 'We just don't get it – you're such a catch, you deserve to meet a great guy' to 'So, when are you going to be the one getting married?'

Finally, I had met someone who would be my partner in everything, including holding a mirror below my nose to check whether I was alive in our advancing years. Yet I had underestimated my parents; they weren't the type to be happy just because I was getting married. They wanted to know the kind of life we would have together; they wanted the measure of Rob.

So what was the measure of Rob at that point? Apart from the parts of him I had fallen in love with, he had told me fairly early on that he had chronic depression. But because I had such a poor understanding of what it was like as an illness, and he was in denial about how ill he could get, I couldn't fathom how huge a thing it would become in our lives.

Besides, at that point, the love in our relationship was a

phoenix: all-consuming and so fiery bright it made any-thing that lurked in the dark seem inconsequential.

So, when my parents asked me, I forgot about the depression. The way I felt was immense, and when it met the counterpoint of how he felt about me, it was as if even the stratosphere wasn't big enough to contain it.

We wanted to be together until the end of our days, have babies, cook meals, spend holidays barefoot and on the beach wrapped up in each other.

Because when you find your big love, isn't that what was supposed to happen?

'He is extremely clever and makes me laugh more than anyone I know,' I said, catching their less-than-convinced expressions. We all stood in silence for a few moments.

'Because,' I said, finally, 'because he is the person I want to spend the rest of my life with. Because I have never been more sure that it's him, and no one else.'

Dad nodded, while Mum went back to inspecting the centipede.

~

No one pressured me into marrying Rob. I didn't go to other weddings feeling a hollow ache that it was the bride, and not myself, on that podium.

My parents always said, 'We want you to be happy.' It was never, 'We want you to be happy and, P.S., can you get your arse moving and find yourself a husband?', like so many other South Asian parents either implied or said outright.

We were a liberal, South Indian family, which included my older sister Priya, who was going through a divorce around the time Rob and I met.

Education and getting a job were considered far higher priorities than tying the knot.

At any rate, marriage wasn't something I was naturally drawn to. Possibly because it didn't seem like married people were noticeably any happier after getting married. But also because I didn't know if I was capable of it, of giving myself and my life to another person in that way.

As much as I railed against bozos I dated who didn't treat me well, full disclosure: *je suis* bozo, because I wasn't always careful with men's hearts. *'Til death do us part?* I was lucky if I could make a relationship last until the next tax year.

And yet, and yet . . .

No one pressured me, but still the pressure of marital love and companionship was all around me. I ate it as a child, I breathed it as an adult. After a while it became the very air I moved around in. There was no depth gauge to measure how deep it went, how purposeful and intense. It commandeered every need and want; it sat quietly behind every thought.

I was seven when I spotted the first boy I ever liked. We were over from England staying with my grandparents in India. As I lurked in the shadows of the apartment block watching him, entranced by this creature, I finally decided to declare my love by tossing a load of heart-shaped pieces of paper over his head from a third-floor balcony. I was so sure he would instantly fall in love with me. Instead, as the hearts fluttered over his head, he just looked confused. As if, well, some nutbag had just thrown a load of paper at him.

I was fourteen when I fell into my first intense, one-sided love affair. A bored, suburban kid from the Home Counties, I was just hitting a stride in my Goth phase when, lo and behold, I came across a boy named Dan, all floppy black hair and Doc Marten boots. Every Saturday, he hung out in a crew of older kids outside HMV in the town centre.

I scoped which bands he liked from his T-shirts, so, inside the store, I dangled myself like a piece of bait in front of the CD racks, in the hope of bumping into him.

'Ah, you too like Cradle of Filth,' I imagined him saying. 'In that case, you must be my one true love. Come, let us away, and snog in the park.'

I unravelled my unrequited love for him across the pages of my diary. I doodled his name on every school notebook.

'I love him,' I breathed to my friends, all similarly kitted out in fishnets, poorly applied eyeliner and garments resembling various interpretations of lingerie.

My bedroom was next to the garage, and frequently I would go out onto the roof to smoke while my parents were asleep. After lighting a Silk Cut like an unholy stick of incense, I would pour every ounce of my being into looking up at the stars and asking them to grant me Dan, because if that happened, I would forever be happy. I wouldn't ask for anything more.

All my woes, from passing my exams to feeling lonely,

would be fixed if he loved me too. Needless to say, Dan did not know I was alive, let alone fall in love with me, but I did pass my exams and won a book prize.

When I met the first man I actually fell in love with, as opposed to stalking him from behind dustbins, I was nineteen. I was the first person he ever loved too, and we marvelled at how lucky we were to have found each other. Our relationship didn't last more than six months, however, because, though we loved each other, we didn't know what to do with it, how to treat each other. We didn't understand yet that love holds respect in one hand, and kindness in the other. Neither of us was happy.

When we eventually broke up, we said goodbye in the softest, most poignant of ways. It was summer, during a break from university. We were hanging out at my parents' house in Kent because they had gone away on holiday. When the time came for him to leave, we knew it would be the last time we would see each other.

I was emotionally exhausted, and he sat on my bed and stroked my hair until I was almost asleep. And then he said, 'In years to come, when you tell people about the first person you ever loved, this was it. Don't rewrite it, don't second-guess it. I loved you, and you loved me. We were the first to love each other.'

When that relationship finished, I didn't pay attention to its ending. I thought we broke up because we didn't love each other enough; I didn't consider that we went wrong in the *way* we loved each other. So, by the time I was in my next relationship, I was already lost in the narrative of love and the excitement that came with it. It was my hair of the dog to all the sadness and discomfort hanging over from my last relationship, and I was only too relieved to find happiness in someone else. This happened over and over again.

And every time something ended, I was left with that same sadness – but also, increasingly, despair. At being lonely again, at having to start over. Because away from trying to establish my career and the sparkle of experiencing urban life through the bottom of a shot glass, I was convinced I couldn't be truly happy without a significant other in it.

In my early twenties, this began as a romantic yearning, and towards the end of the decade, as more and more people paired off, I started to feel an urgent prickle beneath my skin.

No one specifically said the words, 'When you grow up, you are going to have to meet someone, and then you are going to settle down with them and get married and have babies. You are going to need to do this before you turn thirty. And you have to do this because otherwise you won't be happy. You will die alone. And if you don't want to be paired up, then you are weird.'

Yet that doesn't mean it wasn't and isn't implied in every single way we conduct ourselves, in the storytelling around happiness, in the millions of conversations we have over lunch, drinks after work and at family dinners. And if I felt like this as a heterosexual woman, I have no idea how my gay friends felt growing up in such a constrictive framework around happiness.

In life, when you go scuba-diving, down in the depths of the sea, you are given all manner of instruments to survive the pressure of all that water: a regulator, a compressed oxygen tank, a lifejacket that inflates to bring you back up to the surface should you get into difficulty.

But the love that we are taught to expect by right, the story we are told that marriage and kids are a guaranteed route to fulfilment and happiness – how can any of that survive the pressure of real life?

When Rob and I fell in love, it was the deepest love I have ever known. There was no lightning bolt, no dramatic music, but I knew it wasn't like the others. It wasn't teenage love, or desperate and needy love. It wasn't the love of a person desperately seeking the solution in someone else, or love to alleviate loneliness.

It shot up fast like bamboo, yet it had the long, immense roots of a banyan tree, and the feeling we had when we were both together was one of immensity. One of us didn't love the other more; we were gifted the same amount equally.

But I don't know that Rob and I really understood what to do with life once we had found love with each other.

On our first mini-break, to Rome, three months into our relationship, we stayed in a hotel that looked as if it was decorated by an unhinged interior designer obsessed with rococo. We got drunk at the gilt-festooned hotel bar and finally said what was on both our minds: 'I want to marry you and have your babies.' We said this because we knew we wanted to spend the rest of our lives together, and it seemed like the obvious next step. It seemed as simple as:

- Meet the love of your life
- Marry them
- Ideally have children biologically with them; if not, adopt
- Live to a ripe old age together and be happy

It didn't occur to me that anything could go wrong because our love felt so pure, so right and so solid. It felt like the stuff of fairy tales.

We grow up believing that once we have achieved our happy ending, we are guaranteed a happy life. So we believe, in this world that sometimes jolts and cuts us with its rough edges, that it is the lighthouse on the hill. It is warmth and safety; its pursuit and attainment will keep the dark loneliness at bay.

What no one seems to want to talk about is that loneliness exists regardless of whether you are with someone or not. That even with the light of another person casting a glow over you, loneliness within yourself cannot be fixed by the proximity of someone else. But because it's easier to interpret when we see someone going at life on their own, we automatically assume they must be lonely. We say, *This is what loneliness is.*

We don't talk about the times when our partner is lying

next to us in bed, when we can't tell them our fears, when we worry because they aren't telling us theirs.

~

What romcom starts with 'my partner has depression'? What Disney film begins with the princess asking herself the hard questions so that she is prepared for when shit gets tough? Which one ends with the prince saying to her, 'I need help. I don't know if I can do this'?

The glittering bauble of the happy ending is a trap – both in the story it sells, and in the prison it creates for anyone who bought into it and finds life is more complicated than that. And also, because it isn't an ending: it is merely the first act, and yet we base our aspirations around love on an incomplete story, and then wonder why its attainment cannot sustain us for an entire lifetime.

We got married and aspired to have kids because that was the 'normal' thing to want to do, and because we genuinely wanted to do it.

But we also didn't ask ourselves the right questions about the big decisions we undertook, like, for instance, how an illness like chronic depression might affect Rob's role as a husband or our ability to have and raise the kids we so wanted.

About a year after we were married, Rob's behaviour gradually started to change on account of his depression. He had good days, days filled with gardening, films on the couch and big dinners, but he also had bad days. Days spent in bed, withdrawn, quiet. Worries knitted on his brow but translated into words as 'I'm fine' when I asked him about it.

Eventually, three years into our marriage, came the confession: 'I'm not just dealing with depression. I'm also a heroin addict.'

After that, what I thought and knew of love was altered for ever. He also told me the most devastating news, that he had tried to take his own life a few months prior so that I wouldn't find out he had become an addict. So my anger at being lied to flowed in the same deep waters as my concern.

The sense of being betrayed billowed in my chest. But I wanted more than anything for him to feel well and not carry his struggle on his own, so I helped him with his recovery. That's not to say it was easy, or that it didn't come at a huge cost. My sister was the only one who knew for a long time. To the rest of our friends and family, we had to pretend that everything was alright because we were afraid of judgement.

In my most angry of moments: 'I can't believe you lied to me and betrayed our marriage.' In my saddest of moments: 'You've broken my heart.' In my most hopeful of moments: 'We will get through this together.'

Now, I've come to properly understand how formidable a drug heroin is. How much it is moralised, how little is understood about how it affects the mind and the body, drawing it deeper into sickness until using it daily is the only way to maintain a normal life. How it doesn't care whether you are rich or poor, whether you came from a loving family or not, whether you are in banking or on benefits. How recovery is long and difficult.

But back then, I didn't know any of it. I could deal with Rob having depression. I could even deal with the addiction part, even though the road to forgiveness would be long. But at points he seemed so blasé about his recovery and, in the meantime, kept lying about whether or not he was clean and how much debt he was in until I thought I was going mad.

Worse, he could not bring himself to ask for help, despite all evidence to the contrary that he couldn't do it alone and in secret. The final straw was the insistence that he was clean so that we could start trying for children even though he had relapsed on heroin weeks before.

I was so deeply unhappy, I asked for a separation. I needed space to think about what I needed, and whether Rob was capable of being in a relationship. He went to New Zealand to stay with family, while I stayed in London.

I didn't know how I could be without this man, who was so soft in his handling of me, who made me feel like the most beautiful woman on earth even when I looked like something dredged from a drain. But, on the other hand, I didn't know how I could be with him as he was.

I knew then that love wasn't enough. That only Rob could save himself. I knew that as long as we were together, his recovery would only be conducted because he thought he'd lose me, rather than because he was actively choosing it for himself.

While he was still in New Zealand, I told him I didn't think we could work things out, and, eight days later, he killed himself in Auckland.

And this love, this immense love connecting two people like a beam of light, snapped, as one person fell into darkness and the other was left standing at the edge clutching her broken heart, soaked in grief, finding she no longer belongs in the land of living, but not having the courage to follow him to the land of the dead.

~

When you start learning to dive, one of the first things they impress upon you is how important it is to go back up to the surface slowly. You are told lots of important things about pressure, how it affects the body, and buoyancy-control devices.

But when you are actually inside the ocean's belly, it's another thing altogether.

You have been taught the practicalities, but not the poetry of it. Your body slips past the grasp of gravity as you sit, weightless, perfectly caught between two realms.

When Rob was alive, I was too afraid to try diving. It felt too otherworldly; dark and hissing and hidden. But after he passed away, it appealed to me for the same reasons I had found it frightening: I wanted to float in a world that moved in such fluid ribbons of darkness and light.

The first time I tried it, shoals of fish had swum around me in a ball, their silver scales like suits of armour in the light, the dance of lionfish fin rays cast spotted shadows on the sea bed, baby clownfish nestled in pudgy, waving anemones, moray eels stuck their sharp little teeth out from their burrows, bright-purple clams pursed their lips the nearer we floated.

Save for the hiss of my regulator and murmuring bubbles of out-breath, I was enveloped in silence. It rolled over and under our bodies with the current.

Away from the world of starfish and spiky black sea urchins and into the distance, I could sense the susurration of water, the feeling of such vastness out there. As with all places that blurred the lines of existence, wrapped in a valley of quiet where two worlds seemed to join, I felt the skin between my world and Rob's pressing together.

I looked down, the peaceful colour of that world now lost through a gateway of algae and murk. But then I looked up, and saw the surface shimmering, like a dazzlingly bright portal. I knew that when we went all the way to the top, I would feel the sun on my skin, the waves licking my face and, eventually, the hum and tick of my routine back on land: coffee, reading, lunch and maybe a run.

The first year after Rob died could be summed up in that moment of looking back at the surface of a world I didn't belong to. Knowing I wanted to, one day, but I wasn't there yet.

I was living in our rented flat in St Margarets, south London, after he died. My friend Hasiba – or Has, as we call her – moved in with me, and although at first I wasn't sure about living with another person, it helped to have moments when I wasn't in my own head.

I didn't know how I was going to get through the next day, let alone a week, or a year, or a lifetime. It seemed too much to comprehend. So my world became very small and divided into sunrise and sunset – these were the markers I used to get me through one day to the next.

I would wake up and remember. Then I would shower, get dressed in whatever didn't require ironing and go to work. I would somehow make it through the day talking to people, sitting in meetings, and then I would get on the train home. I would fiddle with my Spotify playlist because there is something about grief that completely shits on your ability to read. I would pop into the supermarket, pick something to grill, like a chunk of salmon, and make a big salad.

During the day, my friends would text me, or my parents would call. Everything became small: I could only handle small conversations, small groups of people. I couldn't take on anyone else's problems during this time.

As night fell, I would put on one of Rob's old T-shirts that I had brought back with me from Auckland after the funeral. I would inhale it even though it no longer smelled like him, as if somewhere the fabric and thread were holding the memory of him within. I would get into bed and set my alarm. And then it would come – the wave of it, the crest of a hundred thoughts that he wasn't here, that he would never be here, that I should have saved him, that I couldn't do this without him.

At some point I would fall asleep, then wake up and do everything all over again the next day.

I don't know how I looked to other people – probably fragile, barely there, distant and far away in the eyes. But they knew I was different now. They knew that Rob's death was altering me one painful molecule at a time; only the end result remained to be seen.

I wore the detached look of an observer, because I was. I didn't have a husband, and I didn't have to date other men. My status on kids was unknown; my womb might forever lie empty. I did not have to buy a house, I didn't have to involve myself in petty arguments, I didn't have to attend people's weddings, baby showers, hen dos, kids' parties.

People were amazed when I did basic life stuff like go to work or manage a conversation, so I had dispensation to do whatever the fuck I liked.

That didn't mean the grief didn't bubble out at strange and inconvenient times.

A few weeks after the funeral, I was having a sad day at work. Nothing in particular had happened, but I knew the signs, and I had to leave the office before I started crying at my desk. It was lunchtime, so I decided to distract myself by getting some food, and as I stood in line at our local takeaway place, I started crying. All of a sudden, I heard someone say, 'Deciding what to get, hey?'

It was a male colleague of mine who wasn't exactly known for being soft and fluffy. I tried to stop crying but couldn't, and in the end blubbed, 'I'm just ... *sob* ...

trying ... *sob* ... to decide ... *sob* ... between a chorizo chicken hot box and ... *sob* ... Sicilian meatballs.'

I didn't know if he knew about Rob; I didn't care.

The rest of the time, I just observed life. I didn't have to wonder what direction mine was going in. There was no pressure where I was, only the current curling and uncurling around me, and for a time I was standing motionless, caught between those two worlds.

When Rob was alive, we were under such intense personal and social pressure. We were so worried about buying a house, career trajectories, trying for kids, being financially solvent, presenting a front to the world that we were doing fine.

All of that evaporated when he died. I didn't think of where I needed to be, or where other people *thought* I should be, because those concerns paled into insignificance compared to the need to stay alive. I debated my existence almost every day.

I'm not being dramatic – people bereaved by suicide are 65 per cent more at risk of taking their own life.

This was the best and only thing the grief ever gifted me: what it felt like to be utterly free of the expectations of other people, and, to a deeper extent, of myself.

But at some point the world offers you an ultimatum, because the nature of all living things is to move, grow and change.

So, do you want to be a part of me or not? it asks. And it never stops asking.

Around fourteen months after Rob died, I started to feel the first green shoots of recovery. It started with small things like buying a new bed and sorting through his things that had been kept in the loft.

I started weightlifting because it made me feel empowered but, more practically, I didn't have another person to rely on to flip mattresses or move furniture around. It moved onto bigger things like finally buying my own flat and signing up to online dating.

The surface grew nearer. I wiggled my fingers through that shiny bright portal, dipping back down when the rush got too noisy, too overwhelming. Like a moray eel, I had created a burrow of darkness, silence and peace, somewhere to offset the brashness of day-to-day life.

But these increasingly frequent forays into the real world were making me less of an observer and more of a participant. The more I did things that were a part of it and not the otherworld I had lived in for the past year, the more I was being noticed and drawn into the expectations of others.

Of my own accord, I started experimenting with dating. I wasn't looking for anything emotional, when my head still swirled with the mist of Rob, but I really missed being physical with someone.

'Darling, are you sure it still works?' my friend Martin said.

'Oh, har har,' I replied.

As soon as I started dating the same guy more than a few times, people said, 'Oooh, this sounds promising.'

'Promising for what?' I replied witheringly.

The final straw was when one of my friends, married and with kids, said, 'So, when do you think you're likely going to be in a relationship?'

Was this really how it was going to be? Now that I had finally stopped looking like I was 10 degrees from going batshit, it was fair game to place me back in the sardine run?

While I may have been back in the real world, I wasn't the same person. I was in some ways sadder, wiser, but also my existence was much bigger, more honest.

I could accept a new person into my life, but I didn't need another person to be happy, and that was a critically important distinction.

To be made to feel like I wouldn't ever be *properly happy* unless I was back on that track and seeking those same things again was nonsense.

I realised, once I moved past ranting about being single and happy, that it wasn't just single people who were subject to these narrow expectations. A side effect of speaking so openly about Rob's death, and writing about addiction, mental health and how it affected our relationship, was that people from all walks of life told me a lot of things they wouldn't have normally told others.

They knew I hadn't judged Rob despite everything he had been through, and so if I was capable of that, then maybe I wouldn't judge them. And I didn't.

It seemed as if those expectations never ended, and shunted people towards goals that may not have been theirs.

Whether it's being single, dating someone, getting married, having kids, having *more* kids, and so on.

Are the lives we have the ones we want, or the ones we felt pressured to have? Do we really want those things, or would we have done things differently? What is our own thought, our own hope, and what is the echo of everyone else's?

I needed to figure this out, because the aspiration for the picture-perfect life doesn't prepare you for when things go sideways. It is selling you only half a story, because it implies that when you attain whatever it is peddling, you will be happy. It doesn't tell you that the goal is a shimmering mirage in the desert that evaporates faster and faster as you move towards it. That no one has it figured out, or reaches their deathbed and says, 'Yes, that worked out exactly as I expected.'

The more I swam into the world of the living, the more I was aware that this echo was causing such dissonance. I felt like I needed to paddle faster, to process my grief quicker so I could get back on the baby and marriage track.

I knew it wasn't right, but I couldn't think about what *I* wanted because the echo was what I had been programmed to want since I could remember. It was the collective thoughts and dreams of society, my pre-grief self and everyone around me.

There was my life in London that I loved: nipping into art galleries, putting on smart dresses, talking to smart people. I liked weekend runs along my river, meeting friends for boozy Sunday lunches, driving over to see my mum and dad in the countryside.

But underneath all of that normality lay the memory that still haunts me. It plays over and over again in my mind, and it's as sharp and as clear as the moment it happened. It was the first time I saw Rob in the funeral home.

My best friend Mal had flown over to New Zealand with me. When we arrived at border control, she went ahead of me at the immigration desk. She and the border police looked back at me; I knew then that she was explaining to him why we were over for such a short period of time. I saw the look on his face as it crumpled in understanding.

The weight and comfort of the first hugs as I came out of the airport of John, my brother-in-law, Prue and David. The first glimpse of Felicity's face – Rob's aunt – as we bundled into her home where we were staying for the next few days.

Diazepam. Daylight.

A short drive, or was it a long drive? At any event, a drive.

Meeting Ryan, the funeral director. Being introduced as Rob's wife. Knowing that we needed to pick a casket, flowers, music. The fucked-up diametric opposite of a wedding: no beginnings, only an ending.

Would you like to see him? Yes, more than anything, because all I have wanted over the past twenty-four hours is to be with him. No, because that will make this real.

Seeing him. Not knowing how to even pull language

together to describe the moment, only that my mind doesn't know what it is seeing. It is him, it is not him. Why is he blue? Where is his pinkishness, his almost permanent state of sunburn? Where is the rise and fall of his chest?

What was happening there was loss. But although the shape of this loss was mine – the loss of a partner, the broken dream of love, feeling let down by the world, an uncertain future, intense sadness – it was also a loss so universal that almost every person, in some way, shape or form, has felt its familiar grasp.

And there comes a point, whether through death, loss, illness or heartbreak, when you are forced to take inventory of your life. I loved my life in London, but there were parts of it I wasn't happy with, that I needed to question.

Sometimes the realisation that something needs to change is forced through without kindness or sentiment, so roughly that your whole being is cut up with the violence of it. You look about your life, and you realise that you don't recognise the things in it. They no longer fit the person you are.

Before Rob, I would have let other people influence and steamroll over my own thoughts. But after Rob, after that moment in the funeral home, I realised that beyond the frivolity of YOLO (You Only Live Once), there was something very real about the fragility of living that we seemed to either ignore or take for granted.

I didn't want to live a life of apathy, of regret. But I didn't know how, within the strong tidal pressure of being in London, I was going to figure it out. How life just wouldn't end up rolling into one Sunday lunch after another, grumbling about bad dates and work stuff.

How, before I knew it, I'd be repeating 'Oh, my God, when did it become May/September/December' by the water cooler as my colleagues and I did every year.

When you are in an echo chamber, it is almost impossible to find the frequency of your own voice amid the din and push of others.

3

HELLO, IT'S ME, YOUR WAKE-UP CALL

For as long as I can remember, I've had a job. When I was younger, I was a bizarre little child who wasn't grossed out by feet and, during a time when we lived in India for a bit, I sold pedicures to my grandmother and aunts using a scrubbing brush and the bum bucket. (It's the bucket Indians sometimes use to collect water, accompanied by the bum jug, which ferries the water to wash your behind.)

As I grew older, and we moved back to England, my sister and I used to help out in my uncle Ashok's shop during school holidays.

We lived in the Kent suburbs, while he and his wife Geetha owned a shop in central London that seemed like The Most Exciting Place On Earth.

We were terrible employees: all we did was bag groceries, dust a few shelves and eat about ten times the amount of our pay in chocolates and fizzy drinks as my aunt and uncle gave us free rein of the shop.

Seeing so many different characters pass through those doors was probably why I started falling in love with London. I took it further by sneaking up there as a teenager and going to Goth club nights at the Electric Ballroom in Camden, which seemed witchy and eye-popping.

When I reached legal age, my first proper job started in the butthole of retail: selling double-glazed windows over the phone. It helped fund my trips to London.

By now, my love of London was so deep-rooted there was no question of me not going to university there. While studying English, I worked every Saturday in Selfridges, and my first grown-up job after leaving was working as an intern journalist for a ratty local South Asian newspaper located in a dodgy part of east London. I worked solidly until they offered me a permanent job that paid lower than minimum wage. But it was a step on the ladder.

Although I had always worked for things I wanted – from teddy bears to combat trousers – I was absolutely terrible with money. It dribbled out of my fingers as soon as I got it. But it taught me that, to get anywhere in life, you needed to work hard. If given an opportunity, seize it, be diligent and use your initiative.

A lot of this work ethic comes from my mother and father.

Having immigrant parents is mostly uncool when you're a teenager because they set curfews and threatened to chop the balls off any boys you fraternised with, while your

Western mates roamed the high street at night in miniskirts, Rimmel lipstick and snogged random boys in the park.

I still goggle while watching white parents on TV who let the girlfriends or boyfriends of their teenage kids stay overnight in their bedrooms and then fret about whether they are having safe sex.

Firstly, I wasn't allowed a boyfriend when I was a teenager; secondly, they'd be allowed as far as the living room; and thirdly, my safe-sex conversation with my parents was one line: 'Don't do something that would disappoint us.' And even then, I can't be entirely sure it wasn't about kissing and getting a cold sore.

A bummer when you're a kid, but as an adult, you understood how far their work ethic had taken you.

My mother in particular was insistent that my sister and I always made our own money. 'You never, ever want to rely on a man to provide for you,' she said.

While Dad was doing brutal junior doctor hours in the hospital, Mum worked for Inland Revenue. With two small children, she had to leave the house at 6am, slog all the way to the station, embark on a lengthy commute, do a long day, come home and cook dinner for us.

Both Priya and I had chosen careers as journalists – an industry that didn't pay great – and it's a testament to their open-mindedness that both of them, despite having to work extremely hard to establish themselves, didn't push us into a career such as medicine, finance or law, like many other South Asian parents.

In my case, my report card was so lop-sided in terms of grades, the only way I'd work in any of those industries would be in janitorial services. Priya, however, was very good at science, yet rather than become a researcher or an academic, she became a respected science journalist.

I always knew I was going to become a writer, not because I had a romantic notion of bashing away on a typewriter with pencils twisted in my hair, but because, as early as I can remember, it's what I did. In the same way that reading books was a conduit into wonderful new worlds that I could go and live in for a while, where I trod on their soil and breathed their air, writing helped me articulate how I related to the world.

I wrote stories about being bitten to shit by mosquitoes while on holiday in India. I was the nerd submitting poems for the school's annual yearbook. I received book awards at the end of the school year, and almost every diary organiser since the age of eight had the word 'writer' next to the 'I'd like to be a . . .' statement at the front of every book.

But turning all of this into a career wasn't so evident, and, at seventeen, my goals were flip-flopping all over the place, not helped by my utterly useless career guidance counsellor.

I wanted to be a writer but I also held aspirations of becoming a TV presenter, and while on summer break at university managed to wangle my way onto a niche Asian TV channel through a friend. My job was to present a five-minute fitness segment, which was laughable considering, at that point in time, I smoked like a chimney and did zero exercise beyond lifting pints of beer to my mouth.

For research, I read copies of my dad's *Men's Health* magazines that he kept stashed in the loo. Then I'd drive two hours all the way from Kent to a sprawling white mansion in Hounslow where it was being filmed, smoke a cigarette in the car and then attempt to wheeze my way through plank and mountain climbers.

Sadly, the show never made it to air because of a lack of funding, and presumably because their vetting process for 'expert presenters' such as myself was questionable.

Because I had started out in Asian media, an industry devoid of decent pay, mentoring and career planning – hell, you were lucky if there was even an HR department – I had no idea what I was doing beyond going from one job to the next.

Around four years into my career, I left Asian media and found myself doing a job in mainstream journalism that initially I was so excited to get because it covered the areas I loved – travel, relationships and human interest pieces. But it gradually became evident that the person I was working for was not the best manager.

Meetings were like something from *Drop the Dead Donkey*, the caricature TV programme about a newsroom. You'd get blamed for something that originally started as your boss's terrible idea or bollocked because you left on time.

The final straw was over a little column that fell under my remit, where readers could send in messages for people they'd spotted on the Tube and taken a fancy to. Sometimes people sent in the same message in the course of a week, and although I tried to pay attention to duplication, there were 100 other things on my plate, and remembering that Susan Loves Red Backpack Man was not high on my list.

The editor-in-chief sat me down and explained in a serious tone how he had noticed the same message within the space of a week. He told me how sloppy I was being, and how I really needed to get my act together. I listened to him talking about this column on page 32, which was being used as an excuse to haul me over the coals for a job I worked on twelve hours a day, and I thought, 'Nope, I don't want to do this. I want to travel and not be shouted at for a while.'

In journalism, you are used to a certain amount of sadism, but I was increasingly starting to feel like there was a way you could be in charge and not be a dick about it.

However, being an immigrant's child can have its drawbacks. Ditching your job to go travelling? It's seen as a cop-out. 'It got too hard so I bailed.'

But, actually, I think there is great power in knowing where the line is for you, because I think it gives you an appreciation of your own self-worth, and you can then turn that into something constructive.

Otherwise you go on putting up with a lot of shit indefinitely and become more and more resentful, which inevitably comes out one way or another – whether it's your long-suffering family bearing the brunt of your anger or you end up getting sacked.

So I quit. It turned out that I had made the right choice anyway. Apparently, I was on a fixed-term contract, except nobody had told me that when I got the job, and I was so grateful to be offered it that I didn't press for details beyond my salary. When I handed in my notice, having decided to go to India for three months, I was told by my manager, 'We would've had to end your contract anyway as legally we couldn't keep you on.'

As I stood there with my mouth open, I realised I had learned a valid lesson about what you should be willing to do and sacrifice for work. I had made the rookie mistake of assuming the company was on my side. No, the company is always on the *company's* side.

The trip to India was fun, but being a typical 27-year-old, I didn't learn a huge amount other than that you can catch scabies on a train (this happened to my friend), you shouldn't kiss strange bar owners in Goa (this happened to me) and kayaking through a duck farm is like something out of a horrifying Hitchcock film (also me).

I didn't go outside of my comfort zone; nothing about this trip prompted any form of introspection. I also blew my entire budget within the first three weeks.

When I returned, it turned out that I had chosen to go freelance at the worst possible time: we were entering the biggest global recession since the 1930s.

Work was scarce, so I decided to apply for a permanent job for more financial security. While applying and looking at the measly salary brackets, I had more or less resigned myself to the fact that I was never going to earn big money. In one way it was fine – I had never aspired to make money, and I was so bad with it that I actually came to view my overdraft as my normal bank balance.

'Ms Shetty, would you like to come in to review your finances so we can put a plan together for you?' Lloyds Bank would ask during one of their periodic phone calls.

'Do I have to? I mean is this mandatory?'

'Well, no,' the other person said politely, 'but it might help you in the long term.'

'So, just to check, this isn't because I'm in deep shit with my finances and you're calling in my overdraft because I'm so horribly inefficient with money?'

'No,' they said, half-resigned to what was going to happen next.

'OkaythanksBYEEEEE,' and I hung up.

The more time went on, however, the wider the gulf grew between the finances and lifestyles of my friends, and myself. In my industry, there weren't things like career trajectories or five-year plans.

Beyond the golden apple of the editor-in-chief job, most were standard editor jobs, with varying degrees of responsibility. There certainly weren't bonuses. Most journalists were guided by the dream of one day doing work they were proud of doing, even if it meant being on low pay.

Rather than having friends who worked in similarly beggary creative industries, mine worked in medicine or finance, and while they weren't irresponsible with money, it had stopped being this overwhelming presence in their lives.

They had left the pay-cheque-to-pay-cheque existence back in their uni days.

They spoke of holidays, buying property, wazzing money in restaurants and, for a time, I tried to keep up as best I could, but I was also digging myself further and further into debt.

It was pretty embarrassing when a mate would want to take a cab I could ill-afford and I'd try to squirm out of it, or when they'd all want to commit to some expensive adventure on holiday while I had barely managed to pay for my hotel and flights. So sometimes it was easier to pretend as if the money wasn't real and put it on a credit card than it was to say, 'Sorry, guys, I'm bum broke.'

By the time I had met Rob, I was still piss-poor at dealing with my finances, but I remember feeling comforted by the fact that he seemed to make money easily, and had actually done things with it such as buying a house and going on holidays he could actually afford. We went out for gorgeous dinners, and when we went on holiday, we didn't blow out, but we also didn't scrimp. If I couldn't afford it, he'd pick up the tab.

It seems incredible that this quality that I liked about him, his financial surety, ended up being so heavily commandeered by his addiction. A year after we got married, Rob seemed to be having cash-flow problems. He'd borrow a bit from me here and there, and always return it, but every month it was the same story.

He co-owned his house in Streatham with a friend, and when that friend wanted to sell, we talked about buying another house. But somewhere along the way of house viewings and sketching out whether we needed two bedrooms or three, Rob eventually said, 'Honey, I know this isn't ideal, but I would rather we rented for a year and I can use the equity to pay off my debts.'

I was surprised and a bit disappointed, but I also knew I had debts and no deposit, so of course I agreed.

'How come you have that much debt, though?' I asked.

Rob had managed to rack up a £20,000 credit card bill. 'Wedding stuff,' he replied, which was odd considering I didn't remember him spending that much money on the wedding – my parents and his parents did.

A year after that conversation, he confessed that he was addicted to heroin, so it turned out that the 'wedding' debt was a drug debt, and, worse still, after having used the equity to pay off his bills, he'd gotten himself back into more debt, around £30,000.

In addition to reeling from the discovery that he was an addict, and trying to process how long and difficult it would be to help him through recovery, the debt made me want to vomit.

In that moment, I had never felt so helpless about the amount of money I earned, and how long it would take to claw our way out. I was angry at Rob for lying to me, for the wreck our life had become, but I also saw how the constant worry about money was etched on his face.

In fact, his shame around money, around not being the one to take care of things financially any more, crippled him right up until his death. He loathed the fact that he owed money to people, that he was still cadging off me, but at the same time was trapped in a vicious cycle of using drugs to self-medicate his shame and loathing around it.

He was stuck in what people now refer to as one of the more insidious aspects of modern-day masculinity, where as a human being your entire worth is measured mainly by your economic value. When men can't pull in money or keep up appearances, the shame around it can be deadly because they have been brought up to believe that this is their first and foremost function in life. For Rob, it was a circle of dysfunction that he didn't learn to break.

The fact that I couldn't help financially made me determined to fix my attitude to money. Because what sat on my overdraft or my credit card wasn't play money or imaginary. Money at its most base level represents options, and we had none. It wasn't just Rob who had messed things up; so had I.

Then, while we were in the middle of his recovery, something unexpected and wonderful happened.

By this stage I was working at *HuffPost* and had developed a great relationship with the founder and now ex-chairman of the company, Arianna Huffington. She was championing a message around wellbeing, around how it was as important as pursuing money and power, and we clicked in our united ideals of it.

She has an incredible energy around her, and I'd looked forward to her visits whenever she came over from New York, because after spending about five minutes in her company, you'd come away feeling like you could run the world.

Our editor-in-chief in the UK had just resigned, and Arianna wanted to know if I would help run the business in the UK.

Ohmygodohmygodohmygod I texted my sister, and we screamed excitedly on the phone for about ten minutes.

Overnight, I went from being an editor who was in charge of a little section to the website's number two and the most senior woman in the UK for *HuffPost* while we anointed a new editor-in-chief. I had stock options and an amazing salary.

However, alongside all of this positivity, life was raw and visceral and hard with the effort of Rob and I holding our lives together. For over a year, it felt like the tectonic plates of my two lives were grinding against each other.

The earthquake of his relapses shook our marriage to its core. The aftershocks were steeped in loneliness. I couldn't tell Rob how high a price I was paying to keep his addiction a secret from my loved ones, and I couldn't tell my friends, family and colleagues what was really going on.

Barely three weeks into my new job, we faced a fresh set of challenges. Rob and I lived in a lovely, airy three-bedroom flat in Streatham, but we had finally decided to move to a different postcode because we felt the area was not a great place for his recovery. It was soaked in heroin dealers.

Soon after we moved, Rob had a horrible and cathartic relapse, this time on alcohol. We talked about it and decided the best thing was going to be for him to go to The Priory for some intensive treatment.

'I can't do it on my own,' I cried to Priya when I was at her home in Brighton. She had remarried, to my friend Shabby, and they had just had Leela.

In hindsight, there are a thousand things I wished I had known. That depression is a formidable illness, even more so when its tentacles are wrapped up in the life-sucking leech that is addiction. That we should've gotten more help for him earlier considering how huge his problems were.

While Rob was in hospital, I motored on at work. I don't know how I did, but I managed to keep it together and no one suspected what was going on.

I think I needed work to keep afloat and give me some sense, some hope that there was structure in the world. That I could have a day where I got on the train, muttered dark thoughts at the Victoria line, bickered over the news agenda, agonised over what to have for lunch, bitched about some delightfully insignificant thing with my colleagues.

There is no shadow of a doubt that in some of my most challenging times, work saved me when my personal life was crumbling. So giving it up after Rob died, or not returning to it, didn't occur to me.

Three weeks after his death day, I went back to work.

I didn't know then that a lot of people don't go back to work for a while after a bereavement – six months, sometimes a year, sometimes never. But rightly or wrongly, I didn't give myself permission to do that. I didn't put my grief in a box – it woke up pressing my hand, it sent me to sleep stroking my brow. His pictures were everywhere – the song of his life and his death started and ended each day.

But I knew there was a darkness to it, that the song often felt like it began in the throat of a mermaid, trying to pull me to the bottom. If left alone at home, I would've crawled beneath the duvet and slept my life away.

So I clung to everything light. And at that point, work was light.

Work made me feel like I was doing something useful, especially when I was able to use it as a platform to create discussions around the problems of masculinity that create this desert of emotional silence, and lure men towards suicide. While my personal life was on this strange, rudderless path, like a submarine with faulty engines, work was within my control.

But at some point, the balance tipped. Work was ceasing to be the thing that saved me and, instead, was preventing me from moving forward. I knew I was lucky to have a job that paid well and was sufficiently senior that I was able to make decisions and shape how our business was being run. But being in the midst of it was also hindering my ability to see the bigger picture.

About a year after Rob's death, while still in my

weightless little bubble, I started beavering away on a book called *Chase the Rainbow*. There was so much I wished I had known about mental illness and addiction when he was alive, so much that still wasn't being written about. This was the book I wished I had.

Something to tell me how complex things were, to provide comfort and some sort of explanation as to why Rob found it so impossible to ask for help despite his life falling apart around him.

At the same time, I also had my day job. In addition to the day-to-day running of things, we were understaffed and trying to launch special projects simultaneously.

Emotionally and psychologically, I was reaching an event horizon.

From the outside, I am sure most people thought I was vaguely handling my grief well, because, for the most part, I did my job well. I socialised with people and I was capable of holding a conversation. But the reality was that I was just very good at removing myself from situations when I knew I was going to break down or start crying.

I cried when I ran, I cried just before I went to sleep, I cried when I saw people in love do a delicate dance of kindness to each other, when Crosby, Stills and Nash came on the radio, when I saw bloody meatballs on a menu because Rob had a special pork meatball recipe that only he knew how to make and would never make again.

Much in the same way ahead of the arrival of violent diarrhoea, I felt a tingle that everything was not okay and that I needed to go somewhere quiet to cry or I'd explode.

The end result of this was that once I acknowledged there was a huge set of emotions that I couldn't control, I was ruthless about anything else that made me sad, upset or stressed out that was unrelated to grief.

And although it had saved me once, and I had a big capacity to deal with things that were challenging, my stress levels at work were wobbling dangerously close to making my grief worse.

For so long, work had been a presence in my life that was reassuring and constant. I had worked hard because that's what our parents did, so that's what we did. The goal of work was to have pride in what you did and be good at doing it. But it was also to earn money to build a life, and that life would consist of a partner, maybe some kids. A house in the countryside, holidays somewhere sticky and sweet with ice-cream and sunshine.

But now that this future no longer existed, what was work really doing for me? While I was proud of what I had achieved, it seemed relentless both in workload and the number of fires I seemed to be putting out constantly.

As I listened to people talk about their challenges, career advancement, petty quarrels that would break out over the wrong arrangement of words, I would stare at the ceiling and think: *Did Rob die, and my life get destroyed, so I could sit in a room and defend why someone I manage hasn't replied to an email?*

In my personal life, things were no different. I talked mostly about work, my friends talked mostly about work. We spoke about problems, promotions, bonuses. We never spoke about projects we were proud of, just their final out-come and what that meant to our bank balance.

I had continued with work after Rob died because I didn't know what else to do.

But I knew, when I saw him in the funeral home, that I was learning something extremely important. By the prick-ing of my tears and the cracking of my heart, something much bigger than me was telling me to remember this. That everything in life comes down to this, so I'd better have a long think about what I wanted to have achieved, felt and done by the time it was my turn to lie on that table.

So, clearly, once the mist cleared around my existence, it was evident that some fundamental questions needed to be asked about just what the fuck I was doing with my life.

~

In the movies, life realisations are almost always framed in a dramatic way.

Perhaps time is a factor here: if you don't cut corners, how else can you capture something as complex as the evolution of a human life in ninety minutes?

So it is transmuted into sharp, steep life choices: selling all your possessions, moving across the world, running, running, running towards this future that holds the answer to the sadness in your current life. The problem with this kind of conditioning is that we believe these changes will yield instant results.

Once the risk and the journey are undertaken, we expect the knowledge to drop into our laps arbitrarily, the jewel that sorts our messy lives out and says, 'Lo! I have the solution to your fucked-up life, and if you just follow this plan, you will un-fuck it!'

There is nothing wrong with plans, lists or the aspiration for a life well lived and full of love. But while our existence may be rooted in science and chemicals and numbers, our lives are not mathematics so easily solved by following a certain formula.

When you undergo a life change – whether through experiencing illness, divorce or the death of a loved one – there will come a point when you must gather the blocks of your life and rebuild. There is a hard horizon ahead, in which you will have to confront the fact that the life you had no longer exists.

It was not as simple as leaving my current life and buggering off around the world. Unless you are good at compartmentalising or medicating your life, your troubles, your sadness, your disappointments do not operate to postcodes, latitudes or longitudes.

I knew that a product of Rob's death was that I was learning something far deeper and more profound about the nature of life. But figuring out how I was going to rebuild my life after it was never going to arrive in a thunderclap.

One foggy morning, I was circling the block near my

office. Amid the little blue plaques announcing the lives and deaths of the great and the grimy, this block is well worn by the feet of people working in nearby buildings. A river of stone that has seen a million stress–outs, heard countless bits of gossip about the rise and fall of careers and regrettable office party shags.

Tucked around one corner is a sexual health clinic conveniently placed under a set of damp arches to deal with the consequences of these careless liaisons, while a few doors down is the UCLH Macmillan Cancer Centre.

Now that my grief was marginally less intense, I started to think about my future. And there was a dissonance created by where I *should* be, and where I actually was. The catalyst for all of this was work, which was making me feel like I couldn't breathe. I had spent the past two years since Rob had passed away approaching work at such a full-on pace that I had nothing left to give.

We use that phrase 'burned out', and that is what it felt like. I was a field of scorched earth, a neutron star expected to blaze with light but instead filling rapidly with inky decay.

And so, early one afternoon, I was crying on the phone to Priya. She had spent the past two years in the French countryside commuting to work in nearby Geneva and was an excellent sounding board for perspective outside the London bubble.

Earlier that morning, things with work had been challenging, and I found myself emotional and overwhelmed in the office, in a spot I thought no one could see me. Except a senior colleague did see me and asked me if I wanted to talk.

'You need to brush this off,' he said. 'This is why you have the big salary, this is what you get paid for. You're supposed to be able to deal with this.'

I knew enough about mental health to know that this is the worst thing someone could have said to me. Actually, to anyone. If you're crying uncontrollably, you're probably not thinking, 'Wooo! I'm in total control of my life! I'm a legend!'

You're probably thinking, 'FUCKING HELL, get it together, I can't believe you are this pathetic, this weak, GET IT TOGETHER.' And then along comes someone else, who doesn't have access to your brain, who says out loud the worst things you are already thinking about yourself.

I'm not a person who gets emotional at work, and I'm known for being able to handle large amounts of stress. If things were so bad that I was unable to control my emotions, then it meant I was in distress. Rather than respond to that, what I got was the equivalent of 'man up and get on with it'.

I thought: *Holy shit, this is what guys are faced with all the time?*

Unsurprisingly, this had the opposite effect he intended. I felt like I couldn't or shouldn't express my emotions, yet at the same time they had reached the boiling point of lava.

Rather than erupt inside the office, I walked around

the block to cool off, unable to stop crying. I had written about the need for people to be kind to themselves, to help others who were struggling. And after all that, this is what I was met with?

Yes, I was glad that, after years of being in debt because of Rob and my own mistakes, I was finally earning a decent wage that meant I could spend money on things. But if I was putting myself under such mental pressure simply to get money – what was it all for?

'Pri, I don't know what is wrong with me, but I just can't do this anymore. Normally I can just brush it off and get on with it, but I just can't . . .'

'Poo,' she said gently, 'sometimes bringing in big bucks is not going to make you happy. And if it isn't making you happy, then there's nothing wrong with looking at what else you could be doing.'

As she soothed me and talked me through what was wrong, I saw that I was next to the cancer centre.

I saw a young lady at the reception desk. *Is she a patient or visiting someone?* I saw a family standing outside talking in hushed tones. *Was their world ending or beginning?*

My office was probably 100 metres from where I was standing. While I was upset over problems no one – including me – would remember in a year's time, there was a battle being waged for life here. For the right to spend it with loved ones, to make amends.

For time, for possibilities.

I had both, yet here I was bawling my eyes out. I was

overloaded, overworked. I didn't know where my life was going, and I didn't have the space or, more importantly, the energy to think about it. So when would I think about it? When it was no longer a possibility? When I no longer had time?

Of all people, I should have known better than that.

The realisation that change needed to happen didn't come via a *dun-dun-duuuuuun* moment outside the cancer centre. It had been happening gradually – the pieces of my life pooling together like mercury to spell out a message that I could either heed or ignore.

I knew what happened to people who ignored it – it wasn't pretty, it wasn't kind and it often took months to recover from a breakdown. I knew, by virtue of me having survived two years of Rob's death, that there was a part of me dedicated to protecting me, to looking after me.

She had set my alarm every morning, moved my legs as they ran along the riverbank. She put food in my mouth and willed the blood to flow around my heart.

She had done all of this to get me to the point so that, when the time came, I could make the right decision about my life. To actually choose it, with my whole being, not just survive like a piece of flotsam on the tip of a wave.

I had to heed her.

4

SAND IN THE CRACK OF YOUR EMOTIONAL SWIMSUIT

Escape is not necessarily a bad thing: plenty of us do it by taking holidays to remove ourselves from the humdrum of commuting to work and figuring out dinner.

We wash city filth off in bright-blue swimming pools. We ask the hot sun to burn through our irritations. We unfurl our legs from beneath desks to stride across mountains and sand dunes. But as a long-term solution to an unhappy life, holidays are like trying to sustain yourself solely on air.

You go on holiday to escape being unhappy; you aren't dealing with the thing making you unhappy while on holiday; you return, and are still unhappy, so you book another holiday.

It doesn't help even when you are aware you are escaping your life, as I did when I sometimes took myself off, alone, for a few days to give myself a break from Rob. Although I was terrified of leaving him by himself, I couldn't watch him 24/7, and I needed some time to myself or I'd end up going mad.

One of my favourite places I kept returning to was the Cotswolds. The first time I went back there after Rob told me about his addiction was in January, the off-season.

As I drove down a narrow country lane, the hedgerows strung with snow, I entered a world quiet and hushed. Once I settled into my hotel, I prepared a flask filled with hot tea. I pulled on my walking boots, bundled myself into fleece and wool, and headed out across the fields.

I wasn't thinking of Rob, I wasn't thinking of my friends and family. Here, I didn't have to think. I heard the snap of twigs, felt the embrace of ice and mud underneath my feet, brushed against sturdy green leaves surviving winter, here despite it all.

Overhead, freckles of snow fell softly across the field and I felt my breath, hot and alive, meet the cold winter air as it slowly drew into my body.

It was important because, as short as these trips were, they reminded me a little bit of who I was, and what I liked doing.

It was a respite from wondering if Rob would get out of bed that day, or if I'd have to do the supermarket shop. But it was escape. A temporary reprieve. Being away wouldn't solve my problems or show me a path to happiness.

In the first twelve months after Rob passed away, I spent most of the time wishing I could escape. I wanted to be anywhere but London. I couldn't bear being there.

It changed from week to week; I was going to work in Singapore, Australia, India, anywhere that wasn't fucking London, somewhere I didn't have to scoop up the remnants of my heart every time it shattered because it came across something Rob-like. This initial urge to escape had no form, no proper thought. I just wanted to escape my sadness, do something that would make me feel different, less sad.

As I ping-ponged from one idea to the next, people were sceptical. Looking back, I can see why they didn't really encourage it, because after a soul-shaking loss, you shouldn't really undertake big decisions because a part of your brain loses its ability to think and feel and understand in a multifaceted way.

But in those first twelve months, I was so angry that no one supported my decision to leave to become a yoga teacher or a beach bum. I stopped talking about it and, eventually, I stopped thinking about it. But a full twelve months later – two years after Rob passed away – I found myself in my therapist Isobel's office shortly after my meltdown on the phone to Priya near the cancer centre.

I was telling her about how angry I felt, just all the time, and how I didn't see how things were going to change. I can't recall the exact incident that sparked it, but I must have been telling her that whenever I seemed to want to make a change in my life, people always had opinions on it.

'Okay, so let's look at why this is making you angry,' she said.

I liked Isobel, and I liked the light and airy space in which we talked.

Every so often the inside scenery would change – a pot of lavender here, some linen cushions there. I liked her honesty, the fact that she didn't mind me saying 'fuck' about a thousand times in the space of an hour and, crucially, she didn't irritate me. When she asked that question, I didn't feel the need to defend myself as I did with friends or family.

I was more or less inured to dumb comments around losing Rob, but that week there had been a slew of exceptional donkey-like statements from a number of people, from my hairdresser assuring me I'd meet someone new to someone at a breakfast meeting asking me exactly how Rob had killed himself. Underpinning all of this was about three baby announcements and one engagement.

Finally I said, 'I think it's two things. None of them know what this really feels like. I both envy them that, and resent them for it.

'And by trying to give me advice, or saying that I need to let go, it implies that I'm not doing it right. Or, worse, that there's a solution. That there's a better way to how someone should grieve.

'I know they care. I know they love me – that all this is is love. But I also know that everyone else gets to go back to their lives. They get to plan their futures. And my future has just . . . stopped.'

Isobel looked at me and I knew this dance by now. She knew I had more to say and waited patiently before replying.

I sighed until I found the right emotions and words. 'I feel like an awful person because I'm happy for them. I'm happy for their babies and the love in their lives, honestly. But I also feel like if I'm not presenting this front that everything is fine, I'm not doing my grief right.

'And honestly? I don't know what the right thing is to do. I don't know if I want kids, or if I have it in me to get into another long-term relationship. I feel that everything I do is framed in light of Rob's death.

'Like if I wanted to go to New Zealand for a few months, everyone would assume I'm "not moving on". People forget that I have a whole other family there who I don't see very often. Where Rob actually is spoken about naturally rather than me always having to bring him up in conversation like I do here. And, Isobel . . . I'm fucking tired of it. I don't know what I'm expected to do. I feel like I can't win either way.'

'Well,' she said, 'do you want to go to New Zealand?'

I said thoughtfully, 'I don't know. I feel so peaceful there, like I don't have to pretend. Do I want to go because I feel closer to Rob there? Maybe. But I don't want it to be this place I avoid just because that's where Rob died. I love it *in spite of* being the place he died.'

'Is it a possibility that you can go?' she asked.

I thought of the projects I was working on, the book coming out, uprooting my life, packing up my flat, the amount of energy it would require – the weight of everyone's opinions. I placed my head in my hands and started crying.

'I don't think so,' I replied, snuffling into my fingers. 'I don't see how.'

New Zealand had been on my mind a lot, and not just because of its association with Rob. There was something much bigger than Rob there, in terms of my own relationship with the landscape and how it made me feel.

It began after the first and only time Rob and I went to New Zealand together. We were in a perfectly ordinary part of Auckland – Orewa, along the Hibiscus Coast, where Prue and David live.

Orewa has a long stretch of beach, a wide bar of sand that sits like a lazy crescent moon when the tide is tugged back. As Rob and I walked along the beach holding hands, walking along the edge lined with long shaggy grasses, I felt the blue sky around me, the sound of the sea gathering power as it answered the call of the land to return to high tide.

The imprint of that memory, when air, sky, land and water met, would act as a beacon for whenever I needed peace. I would remember it in meetings, or when I felt the city was becoming too argumentative to be in. I'd hold it close whenever I felt trapped and unhappy or filled with noise.

It was the first time I experienced a place that gave me such a sense of quiet and calm. Long after I returned to England, I carried that feeling inside me and pressed it to my heart.

'Sometimes,' my brother-in-law John said, when we were both looking out to the ocean a few days after Rob's funeral,

'I think all I need to feel peaceful is to watch the light on the sea. I know it sounds silly but . . .'

It didn't sound silly; I knew what he meant.

After Rob died, I went back to New Zealand nine months later as part of my healing process around his passing. I went to a number of places, and in each one I felt the frequency that truly peaceful places emit, their sound created in the lapping of waves and the language of birds.

Time moves differently in these places; it slows, becomes elastic, and it winds itself around you until all the urgency in you is cried out.

When my dad looked at the pictures I took while I was there, he used the nickname he had for me since I was a baby and said, 'You look very peaceful here, Putta.'

I needed to restore that sense of peace, but I didn't know where to begin.

'Okay, let's think about this a different way,' said Isobel, after I had gone through the better part of her Kleenex Mansize. 'If you just kept going, and everything in your life is exactly the same in six months or a year's time, how would you feel?'

I knew what it was like to be pinned at the bottom of the ocean by sadness so heavy all I could do was blow bubbles of air and hope for the day when it lifted. I knew that nothing I could do would make it happen faster; it had to happen in its own time.

But now, I had choices. Even if I didn't feel like I had choices, I did.

The prospect of staying in my job, doing the same thing day in, day out, watching other people's lives move forward while I was still prodding the edges of my heart figuring out whether it could withstand the rough currents of dating, going to dinners, watching Netflix, getting drunk, going to Christmas parties and summer parties – it was as if I was back at the bottom of the ocean, except this time, someone was holding my nose. I felt like I couldn't breathe.

'I couldn't bear it,' I whispered.

'So what do you want to do?'

I knew the answer was travel but the words stuck in my throat because it sounded flighty, frivolous – a cliché. Yet I knew enough by now to know that this wasn't about escaping my sadness. This wasn't about going to live in an ashram in India or a hermit shack in New Zealand to jumpstart a newfound appreciation for my life.

Plus, I am too Indian for that. Although I'm British born and bred, I visit India every year. I even lived there for five years as a kid when my parents decided we were going to relocate there.

'No fishfingers?' I said before we got on the flight, clutching my BA kiddies' flight pack filled with crayons and colouring paper.

'No fishfingers,' my mum replied. 'But you will have a renewed sense of cultural identity and that will be just as tasty, won't it?'

My seven-year-old self strongly disagreed when she realised it was going to be curry for breakfast, lunch and dinner, and the bright hope of fishfingers was replaced with a very quick understanding of how disposable life was.

While I was carted around like Little Lord Fauntleroy in Mum's little red Maruti car, children with hair the colour of straw clambered over the waste in huge open dustbins. Being wasteful or picky about dinner wasn't an option when food was the pressing concern for so many. Conversely, I also learned how, despite having nothing, a lot of people still celebrated life and got on with it.

I didn't use their poverty to make me feel better about my life, I just had a better understanding than my English mates, when we came back for secondary school, that life is complicated. It ebbs and flows; there is joy and sadness, food and hunger, and if you are in a position to do so, you help those who need help.

For as long as I can remember, after family parties or when we couldn't eat all our food in one go, it would be parcelled up and given to the maid or the night watch-man. Nothing was wasted; everything moved and turned in a circle. I'm still horrified at the amount of food I see people tipping into their bins or those who think noth-ing of over-ordering food at restaurants and seeing it go to waste.

So I didn't need spiritual awakening. I didn't need travel to save me or show me how lucky I was. This was about me taking my life in my own hands and willing this new version of myself into existence.

'I need to leave,' I said to Isobel, but because my

nose was so bunged up from crying it sounded like 'I neeb to lieb.'

Isobel nodded. 'Good,' she said.

I looked at the damp tissue in my hands. How many tissues had I filled with my sadness in the past year? *Enough*, I thought, *enough*. I could live with crying because I missed Rob. I couldn't live with crying because I was too much of a coward to take control of my life.

'I'm not . . . I'm not leaving because it's too hard to handle or I'm escaping,' I say, more than anything, because I need to believe it. 'I'm leaving because, for the first time in my life, I am actively choosing to think about what I want from my life, and I can't do that here.'

She murmured her understanding. I eventually lifted my head to finally look her in the eyes.

'I'm like that apartment in a building after a massive earthquake. Everyone else's apartments are fine, but mine is the only one shaken to smithereens.

'I'm trying to rebuild, but I know it will never be the same. And that's okay; it doesn't need to be. It survived an earthquake; it's still standing. So somehow, I have to make peace with the fact that it will never look the same as all the others, but that's what makes it stronger.'

~

Here's the less glossy truth about trying to make a decision when you are in the middle of a mental crisis: it is fucking hard.

Not all breakdowns happen instantly, such as not being able to physically move from the top level of a bus or losing the ability to speak. Some happen slowly because you trick yourself into thinking you're fine. Every time your body and mind send up a distress signal, you tell yourself it's just a drill; it's not the real thing.

By the time you've reached a stage of snot, tissues, losing your shit in Starbucks because they've yet again spelled your name 'Prawna', you are at a difficult point. You are in an advanced state of erosion and pieces of you have worn away without you even noticing.

The reason it's hard is because your ability to reason and make decisions is shot to shit. You need a resolution, quickly, or more and more of you is going to crumble off.

Even if your ability to make a decision isn't corroded, it's still hard to overcome the fear of it being a terrible decision. Around this time, I started getting into podcasts, and one of the first I listened to was called The Unmistakable Creative, which featured a guest named Dr Srini Pillay, assistant professor of psychiatry at Harvard Medical School.

By coincidence, he was talking about change, and said that the brain is actually wired for change but resists it.

'The moment you say, "Hey, I want to go to the gym," your brain is pretty onboard with it because it's an idea,' he says.

'Then when you actually make that effort to go, the moment your brain knows you are committed to an action, it actually starts creating brain chaos, which we call

cognitive dissonance. And when there is cognitive dissonance, the brain goes back to what it was doing previously,
so that it doesn't have to deal with that chaos.'

I had decided to quit my job and leave, but my brain
was certainly in chaos, and it took daily reminding that I
was doing a good thing despite the screeching uncertainty
ahead. What didn't help was that some people said, 'Wait,
you're leaving your amazing job and your life in London
to go travelling? What if you don't find a job when you get
back? Are you going to be okay financially?'

In that same podcast, Dr Pillay talks about the 'switch
cost', so, basically, this is the psychological price you pay for
changing your life. A lot of people go 'nah' and don't make
the change because the cost is often uncomfortable; you feel
anxious, less certain, fearful. It's the equivalent of wearing a
wet swimsuit with sand lodged up your crack. You wriggle
and wriggle but you can't get comfortable.

Even if you manage to overcome this, other people find
a way to project their own concerns onto you.

Eventually, I succumbed to self-doubt. What if I didn't
get a job when I returned? What if I ended up back in the
debt I had worked so hard to get out of? What if I was just
putting my life off indefinitely?

Someone who writes a lot about the path to mental
wellbeing and unravelling some of the big questions we
have about our lives, from loneliness to happiness, is Oliver
Burkeman, who writes the weekly 'This Column Will
Change Your Life' for *The Guardian*. Interestingly, he's also

published a book called *The Antidote: Happiness for People Who Can't Stand Positive Thinking.*

I asked him about his advice for people making life changes when they were really afraid of change.

He told me that courage or bravery was not to do with not feeling afraid. The difference, he said, was 'acting, while feeling afraid'.

Leaning into that initial fear was part of the magic of making a life change. So, in effect, although your brain senses fear and takes that as a sign to avoid change, changing your perspective to expect to feel fearful – and accepting that it's perfectly normal to feel like that – is what will help you carry it through.

Plus, just understanding that not every change you make is for ever. Life is rarely a dramatic novel where one small action causes a tragic spiral of events – most things can be course-corrected and tweaked.

The fear that was being generated inside me was feeding off everything in the past: the times I'd found it difficult to secure freelance work, the fear of being broke again. This, despite clear evidence to the contrary that if I'd managed to do it once, I could do it again.

Despite the doubts, once I decided to leave, it was almost theatrical how much better I felt. The things that had previously seemed impossible were actually easy to solve. While abroad, I could work freelance when I needed money, rent out my flat and do it on a short lease in case I wanted to come back early.

I spoke to people who seemed like they might under-stand. We expect all the same things from our friends when, actually, we are friends with different people because they speak to and resonate with a particular aspect of ourselves. Trying to get validation from people like my friend Aman or those who would never dream of risking their livelihood to go surfing in India was wasted breath.

Priya was one of my favourite people to talk to, because she knew what it felt like to have to rebuild your life, having gone through a divorce. And because, being my sister, she didn't indulge in polite fripperies.

'For what it's worth,' she said, 'I think it will be good for you, and I think you need to do it.'

I also talked to my old colleague and friend Craig, who had announced on Facebook that he and his wife and two young kids were going to leave England for an open-ended trip to Southeast Asia, Australia and New Zealand, which was a minimum five months away. They also kept their cir-cumstances flexible in case they didn't want to come back.

I pinged him on Facebook Messenger to ask how he planned it. 'The aim was pretty clear,' he wrote back, 'which was a compelling adventure with family, exploring new places. But we also wanted to create a situation where we could decide new career paths and answer two straight questions: Where should we live? What should we do?

'From decision to departure was six weeks, which didn't give people much time to react. But there was a mixed reaction from family and friends – family I was travelling towards were delighted, those we left behind were saddened but supportive. Friends were a mixture of supportive tinged with jealousy, with – I expect – elements of scepticism, i.e. "You'll be back". All are perfectly understandable responses.'

I asked him what he and his wife were hoping to achieve by it, and he said, 'We're deciding on a new career path and a new home for our family, and I think whatever the outcome it won't have been brought about by the opinions of those around us.'

I experienced something similar, although admittedly I didn't have to factor in three other people. After the initial shock for people wore off, and they realised I'd already made the decision, we started having proper conversations about it.

The more this happened, the more I realised that in some way or another, everyone is wondering the same thing about their own lives.

Is my life what I chose consciously and independently of anyone, or what I chose unconsciously based on the choices of other people?

It doesn't matter if you're straight, gay, trans, bisexual, black, white, brown, married, not married, divorced, open relationship, with kids, trying for kids, can't have kids, don't want kids – fundamentally, we all want a fulfilling, peaceful and happy life, with our loved ones safe and sound.

I was talking to my friend Peg about it while we were having lunch at a horribly expensive Mexican small plates place. (What is it with the urban obsession about small plates? I feel like I'm spending twice as much to eat half as much.)

'I totally get it,' she said. 'There is this whole expectation and pressure to be a certain way or aim for a certain thing, and by the end of it, you don't even know if that's what you want.'

Peg is divorced and is bringing up her eight-year-old daughter alone, while her ex-partner is remarrying.

'I mean Mark is remarrying, and good for him. We were miserable. But there are all these big eyes looking at me with pity, you know, like I'm the one worse off because I haven't met someone yet and I'm not settling down.'

Peg, like a lot of other people who go through divorce, was emotionally walloped by it. On the one hand, she was relieved to no longer be in a relationship with someone she didn't want to be with. On the other hand, nothing prepared her for the awful sense of loss, and the grief around her marriage.

As well as mourning her future with this person she thought she would be spending her life with, she then had to deal with navigating her way through her old social circles while grappling with the newer parts of herself.

'Right,' I replied, 'and the thing is, we're wise to this shit. We've experienced marriage. It's not the easy, quick fix to a happy life. So why does everyone keep pushing it as if it is?'

One of our mutual friends, Jess, joined us about an hour later and asked us what we were talking about. We filled her in, hesitantly at first. Jess has an enviable life in West Hampstead with one beautiful little girl, a recently refurbished house and a gorgeous husband.

'Look,' she said, taking a glug of her wine, 'I know I'm

lucky. I know I have the husband and the kid, but it's not all it's cracked up to be. Married people do not tell you their problems. So you think they don't go through it, or that it's more idyllic. And trust me, I love being married, it's rewarding when it works. I get to go through the best and the challenging times with my best friend at my side. But I also know it doesn't stop there. That there isn't still stuff that . . . doesn't work out the way you want it to.'

Peg and I listened but didn't say anything. We both knew Jess and her husband had been trying for a second baby and hadn't been successful. Jess had been having a rough time of it with two miscarriages.

'People have been asking me if we're going to give Anna a sister or a brother. You know, because it's as easy as buying one from a supermarket.'

If you looked at Jess's Facebook or Instagram account, you wouldn't be privy to any of this. You'd see a perfect life, a perfect home, a perfect marriage.

There's an old saying: don't compare your insides to someone else's outsides. While social media fuels a lot of the yard-measuring of perfection at a much more frequent and intense pace, it always existed.

It reminded me of a column Oliver wrote around the concept of loneliness, basically saying that the problem with repeatedly witnessing people's social events is that you usually do it when you're in solitude. Therefore, it underpins this belief that you are on your own, while the rest of the world has their shit sorted.

When I spoke to him to ask about change being so scary, and how a big part of that was driven by the concern that I'd be left behind in my life and career if I just absconded for eight months, he reminded me of a really important thing.

'We are so accustomed to comparing ourselves to other people and not taking into account that we have unique access to one mind full of emotions and thought, and no access to everyone else's emotions and thoughts,' he said.

'In a way, in an existential sense, you are inevitably on your own in that respect no matter how great a network you are in. There's something about being you that can never be communicated completely to anybody else.'

Yet, despite this, despite being the only person to fully comprehend our own worries and wants, we allow other people's emotions and opinions to govern what we should be doing, how we should be thinking.

Caught between the external current and our internal flow, no wonder so many of us feel lonely within our own lives.

~

Around two weeks after seeing Isobel, on New Year's Eve, I was starting to make dinner for myself in my flat, alone. Earlier that day, I'd gone to my favourite cheese place, selected the juiciest beef fillet from the butcher and picked out an incredible Barolo.

'You're spending it *alone*??' people said.

'Yep,' I replied.

When I was a teenager, I loved the promise of New Year's Eve – it was an excuse to pilfer the reject booze from our parents' liquor cabinets.

But quickly, I learned the truth: that the idea of it was always more beautiful than the reality.

My first unsupervised one was a dodgy house party in my hometown of Dartford – a place once known for its leper colonies and smallpox hospitals, now for pound shops and as the birthplace of Mick Jagger. I wondered why people were putting talcum powder on a mirror. (Reader, it was not talcum powder.)

I remember starting the evening feeling thrilled at the prospect of glamour and freedom, and finished it feeling let down, cradling a box of chicken nuggets.

The last New Year's Eve I spent outside my own home was with Rob before I knew he had an addiction problem, with a group of friends in a pub. It was in a sad, grubby part of Farringdon; we ended up getting kicked out ten minutes before midnight because someone had started a pub brawl.

'Never again,' I said to Rob as we sat in the taxi on the way home.

When he entered into recovery the next year, we stayed in out of necessity and because we didn't want to pretend to others that the following year was going to be The Best Year Ever. We knew that though we loved each other, though we hoped it would be a better year, it would still be a tough year until we felt more stable. Those last two years we shared were quiet, beautiful and we ended each one with a kiss.

For my first New Year's Eve living alone, I realised I didn't want to spend it with anyone else. I wanted to cook some great food, watch a film. I wanted to wake up the next morning and go for a run in the crisp first hours of the New Year.

I didn't want the forced sense of celebration that comes relentlessly, the too-bright fun of people drinking and raised voices. For me, this night was about taking in all of the wonderful things I had done, and, above all, it was a time for me to remember my life and all that had happened.

At midnight, I lit a candle. I opened the window and breathed in the winter air.

I said hello to Rob, told him I loved him. I said I would always love him and that I hoped he knew I was approaching something like happiness. That he wasn't to worry. That I wished him peace and love, always.

The softness of that night rolled through the window, the quietness came down upon the room and wrapped me in all of the emotions that painted Rob in my mind. In that moment, I felt how sharp the balance was between my existence continuing or winking out. I knew, then, that in deciding to leave, I had made a choice for my survival. To move forward, not escape.

Then, in the distance, the stillness was pierced with the sizzle and crack of fireworks, and just like that the flame flickered, and the real world poured in with the smell of frost and gunpowder on its breath.

~

The next morning, after my New Year's Day run, while sipping tea in my living room, I thought about where to go on this journey I had now set in motion. I closed my eyes and felt the perfect balance between the past, present and future.

I thought of all the places I had ever loved, where my mind felt free, and my edges were softer.

One of these places was Kerala, in South India, where the landscape is woven in coconut trees, where waters of the Arabian Sea mix with the Laccadive Sea that borders Sri Lanka.

Along the many waterways that dissect the south of the state, the backyards of houses dip straight into the surrounding lakes, depositing children having a wash, women thudding clothes against well-worn stones, and families trooping up and down sedately in canoes.

My favourite thing to do when I am there is kayaking. The year Rob died, my parents and I went there to spend time with each other, and to escape the first Christmas of him not being there.

Kerala shares similarities with the neighbouring state my family comes from: Karnataka.

Our family kitchen tables are strewn with tamarind, fish and coconut. Our bodies remember a time when our ancestors slipped in and out of the water. Our skins range from almond to the most beautiful indigo blue.

After I waved Mum and Dad goodbye back at the hotel, their eyes heavy with concern about whether I would be okay, I hopped into a taxi to take me to the water's edge.

And as I eased into my kayak, it created tiny ripples that shifted underneath the carpet of water hyacinth that clogged parts of the waterways with thick, fat leaves and purple petals. I liked to kayak in the early morning, to try to beat the sun before it clambered up to its highest point, searing every open inch of earth.

The first few strokes of the paddle warmed me up, slicing into the water, until its rhythmic, familiar sound became a mantra. *Swish, splash, swish, splash.*

The first people I came across were always fishermen, waiting for a small catch to sell to market vendors who positioned themselves near a string of houses for a quick and easy sale.

The fish unique to Kerala is the *karimeen* or pearl spot fish, flat like a pancake with a black spot on its side. My stomach remembers it covered in turmeric and chilli, fried in the comfort of someone's home, served alongside hot fluffy rice and soupy dal.

In that newborn, pink light, the lake spread out like a clear mirror, its slow, deep heart thudding against the banks. Kingfishers zipped along the waterway, while snake birds rearranged themselves into their distinctive shape to dry off their wings.

When I got far enough that I couldn't see the river-bank, everything started to shuck away – the fishermen, the little children in neatly oiled plaits heading to school, the inquisitive housewives and retired old men wondering what an Indian woman was doing paddling into the heart of nowhere.

'Isn't she worried about getting dark in this hot sun?' I could hear them think.

When the British packed up and left, they unknowingly planted in the bosom of the Indian subcontinent a diseased obsession with fair skin. Economic emancipation from the colonial days may be underway, but, psychologically, it will take a lot longer because, to most South Asians, fair still equals beautiful, dark equals bad. We can't do anything about the amount of melanin we are born with, but boy do some of us try.

I didn't care about my skin getting darker in the sun, never have done. There's no way a fiery ball of gas or weird colour prejudice is going to limit or dictate what I can or can't do.

I remember the silence deepening the further I moved away from people, and when I hit the centre of it, I lifted up my paddle. I heard the last few drops of water hit the surface of the lake, the rustle of coconut trees shaking their leaves out like a bunched-up skirt.

Turning this memory over in my mind on that New Year's Day in my living room, I wondered what it would be like to do this in Karnataka, to feel the bones of my ancestors rising up through my feet.

Because, in that place of quiet in Kerala, I wasn't thinking of my family or my friends. I wasn't even thinking of Rob or future loves waiting in the wings. As I sat on my sofa, I recalled that moment for what it was, and how it smelled like sun and river water and emptiness.

~

Once I handed in my notice, the pace began to quicken. I had to tell my then book editor Nicki about my plans to leave and gave her my reasons. 'Why don't you write about it?' she said.

I squirmed: wasn't it a bit *Eat, Pray, Love*? I didn't have a vendetta against the author, Elizabeth Gilbert, but her book – while it helped a lot of women – turned the travelling-to-find-yourself book into something of a cliché.

Her experience is held as a template for transformation that will burn through unhappiness, and I think there is a danger in relying on something other than yourself to fix what's wrong, or the belief that something will swoop out of the murk to make sense of all the chaos.

Plus, I wasn't travelling to find myself; I was travelling to get lost in myself. 'Well, write that,' Nicki said.

The first self you are given is often taken for granted, the making of you formed when memory wasn't yours to command yet.

It is built from the thoughts and actions of everyone you've encountered so far, including your parents, your experience at school, your friends, and your journey into adulthood. It is all your first times. Its construction was so long ago, you've forgotten what it is made of.

But when the earthquake has come, and you are forced to rebuild from the rubble, your second self is more awake, aware, careful.

I made a heart from what was left of the remnants, and what other people gave to me in love, willingly. I made a body from running and lifting weights because it was the only thing that gave me respite. I made a soul from the love and sadness Rob left me with, and the strength I earned just by agreeing to be in the world every day.

My mind took the longest. At first, I protected it by doing only what I felt capable of. I reduced every action and thought to its simplest form: eat, sleep, breathe. And when it was ready, I looked at its shattered fragments and I looked at the person I wanted to be, and in the quiet of my own home, I stitched together the parts of myself that had survived the fire of my grief. Stronger, vaster, more complicated and resolute.

It is not transformation through pasta and preaching; it's the transformation of wolves. Piercing the silence of your loss is the crack and break of sinew and bone, it is the river of blood that flows around all of the blasted remains of your former self, because you are changing all of yourself to become something altogether more powerful, more truthful.

I arrived at this point because I went to that precipice of life and death every day, where my mind was torn apart and put together *every day*. No one said, 'Hey, champ, take some time off from navigating the alleyways of insanity and reality.' I did it while buying milk from Tesco, signing off an invoice, going to people's birthdays.

This trip wasn't a gimmick. It wasn't about travelling the world in a kayak I made myself or staying with Finnish ice carvers.

Each of these places would have to *mean* something. So Italy and Thailand wouldn't make the final cut because they just seemed like nice places for a holiday.

When I sat down to draw up a plan of where to go, India was at the top of this list.

There was no point me going to Peru, for instance, because there are no other versions of me in Peru. I didn't cycle into a foot-high pile of cow dung there (true story), or drop heart-shaped notes on a boy's head. I didn't cry behind its trees or learn about how awful girls could be to each other. I didn't learn how to cook or become afraid of heights there.

To a certain extent, figuring my stuff out means looking at the type of person I used to be, looking at the person I am, and working out what needs to change, and what needs to stay the same.

I've long since realised – especially in matters of India – that there is a distorted perception of what it's like as a place versus the reality. You arrive expecting exaltation; you leave feeling hot and sweaty, feeling like you don't quite get it, but *everyone else got it*, so maybe there's something wrong with you.

Or you are fully suckered by the travel reviews. There have been plenty of times I've gone to some 'must-see little place that serves the best meat curry' to find it's literally a tin-pot, dime-a-dozen shack, or braved the heat to see the flower market with its 'dazzling colours'.

Five minutes in, you've seen one marigold, you've seen them all. Flies settle on your skin. There is a child tugging at your trousers. You're getting hot and sweaty. One day it will turn into an anecdote you tell your friends about 'crazy India'.

India is so much bigger than that. She has vast deserts where the dreams of camels roll across the dunes. Her seas are beautiful and wild, and she snacks on swimmers who underestimate her terrible and quiet fury.

Her mangroves flow across the lips of riverbanks and spread into a tangle of leaves and roots, hiding tigers and crocodiles within their folds. Her eyes look out from languid pools framed in the twist of forests; her back is the snowy arch of the Himalayas. She has silence within her, but it gets lost in noise because that makes for a more interesting travel feature.

Although India is a place I usually visit to hang out with my relatives and get drunk on beer, I felt she was an important place to visit. She was my past, but she was also my future. In order to figure out the mechanics of myself, I needed to do that within her landscape, because there was a part of the old me from before Rob died who was still locked away there and hadn't yet grieved or made her peace with the loss and this new person she was becoming.

Nepal seemed like an obvious choice because her mountains were unlike any other in the world: austere beauty met with warm and friendly people.

New Zealand was a contender because she had already begun her siren call. She thumped her fist at me from beneath the seabed, she crooked her finger and pointed towards her corridors of mountains and glacial lakes. I frequently saw her in my dreams. Never Rob, only her.

New Zealand and India also meant fulfilling a promise to myself: to spend more time with my parents and Rob's parents. None of us wanted to say it, but they were all getting older, and I didn't want our relationship to cruise on the autopilot setting we have reserved for our parents.

After visiting those three places, maybe I would be more at peace with being home in Britain. I didn't expect to fix my sadness, but I wanted to create an inner reservoir of calm and quiet that I could draw on whenever I was in need.

What was this about? It was about belonging. But not the belonging of a hermit crab; I wasn't looking for pieces of another person's shell to stick to my own.

What was this about? It was about love. But not about love that rescues; I was trying to honour the relationships I had and trying to survive the most important one I had lost.

What was this about? It was about strength. But not strength from an invisible saviour, strength that originated within myself and came from the people already in my life.

What was this about? It was about expectations. But working out the ones other people have of me, the ones I have of myself, and the ones I want to work towards meeting.

What is this about? Well, let's begin.

5

Love, But Not as You Know It

There's a period of dead time, between your old life and your new one, where you are thinking WHAT THE FUCK HAVE I JUST DONE?

Especially if you have done something foolhardy like try to save money by temporarily moving back in with your parents. My rationale was that as I'd be leaving mid-month in September, there was no point paying for a full month of my mortgage.

'Hang on,' Mal said when I called her up, lying on the floor in my bedroom like I did back when I was fifteen to discuss boys, Silverchair and The Note Brooke Passed In Maths. 'Haven't you only been there five days?'

'What kind of best friend are you?' I replied. 'It feels like it's been FIVE YEARS.'

To get to my parents' house, you drive along the M25 and turn off into country lanes, along tarmac pressed at the feet of trees and hedges until these shadowed avenues of leaf and branch open into fields of rapeseed, igniting the landscape in a blaze of yellow.

When I was a child, I itched to escape this place. I looked at the fields and saw only their borders. I wanted noise because the silence was deafening. I tried all manner of tiny and pathetic rebellions: smoking cigarettes in cornfields (I got bitten by ants); my first tattoo (at a place called Kev's Tattoo Parlour, which had a beaded curtain instead of a door); and my first kiss aged fourteen with an older metal-head boy named Mark (he had long curly hair and kissed like the Facehugger from *Alien*).

As far as South Asian parents went, mine were pretty liberal. As a kid, I was never going to have the freedom of my white friends, who were allowed to roam the high street at all hours.

But I went to sleepovers, dressed how I wanted and went to gigs up in London despite the concept of a gig being utterly foreign to my parents because they had both grown up in India. Not once did they say, 'We're not sure about this Marilyn Manson chap and his dodgy eyeball.' They never told me what to study, or who to become.

The natural order of the parent–child bond is that you all love each other unconditionally, but you, as the child, don't make a huge amount of effort with your parents. If you're middle-class and comfortable in your love, you visit them on the weekends, expect to be fed like royalty and then you slob on their sofa until it's time to go.

Maybe this is how it would have been. But our bond

deepened and strengthened because of what I went through with Rob. When he was alive, there was a lot I didn't tell them – specifically about his addiction – and when he died, I was in their home the day I got the phone call.

They had been there unconditionally, and even when they must have wanted to ask a thousand questions, they didn't pressure me with it. After he passed away, I didn't want to live with all of the secrets that had burdened my life for so long.

Once I confessed what had happened, they didn't judge me, and they didn't – despite my deepest concerns – annihilate Rob's memory. It sounds so silly, but I was so scared that we wouldn't be allowed to talk about him. Instead, they hugged me, gave me understanding, and that moment remains the time I have felt most loved by them.

We have a good relationship because we've had to work at it.

I was finding it challenging being back in their house, but it wasn't because of anything they did. Mum was adorable and kept trying to feed me, while Dad the resident bartender was always game for a glass of wine – 'It's five o'clock somewhere' being the motto on the family crest. It was more about the cognitive dissonance being created by my life choice.

Everyone kept saying, 'Oh, my God, is it amazing that you've left work?', but it's not like the rewards instantly kicked in. You don't dance around like Maria in *The Sound of Music*, and actually, if you did, it indicates you had a

Love, But Not as You Know It

fucked-up and dysfunctional relationship with your job. It wasn't always perfect, but I loved my job.

Rather, it was the transition from one state to another, and what didn't help was that, mixed in with all this doubt of 'What Have I Done?', I had unwittingly moved to a place where I instantly regressed – because that's what you do when you're in your parents' home. It fed into this feeling that I'd made a bad choice and was going backwards, not forwards.

If an edifice could be a metaphor for my emotional turmoil, it would be the New Ash Green Shopping Centre, an awful collection of buildings built on an architectural blueprint of mediocrity, tucked away in the middle of nowhere.

In the decades my parents lived in the area, I had never heard of this place, yet mysteriously it was only a five-minute drive from their house. Clearly it had been clinging to the underskirt of their life like an unwanted mushroom.

'Come on!' my mum said. 'I must have told you about it.'

'Nope,' I said adamantly. 'Trust me, I definitely would've remembered this festering shithole.'

I had only stumbled across it because I was looking for a cheap gym near their house. But there was something oppressive about it, a certain funk, as if everything had been placed here and left to rot like an egg and cress sandwich stuck behind a radiator.

There was a bakery that sold bright-pink iced buns and unfulfilled ambitions. An estate agent touting new beginnings alongside tired homes trapped inside pebbledash. A

89

defunct bank with wooden planks nailed over the doors and windows. A charity shop selling Katie Price books, polyester knitwear and a dead grandma's crystal set. A tanning salon with a solitary receptionist who was the colour of Fanta.

The gym was possibly the worst I had ever been to. It wasn't even that the weights of the dumbbells were written on them in Tippex, but the clientele made me think, 'Holy crap, is this my peer group now?'

Two scrawny students with hair gel and Lycra man leggings. One middle-aged man in a moustache wearing 1970s running shorts. Five old ladies in varying shades of pastel leisurewear. One guy around my age who looked so sad I was certain he was going to start weeping on the Leg Curl.

I hyperventilated, bought an iced bun and sat in my car. Everything I owned was now in storage, and I had reduced myself to living out of a suitcase for the foreseeable future. Soon, even the car I was sitting in was due to be sold. Was I going to end up like these people, weeping in a forgotten wasteland filled with bad tans and frustrated lives?

I punched the button on the car sound system. Srini Pillay, whose podcast episode I kept listening to on repeat, reassured me through the airwaves that feeling uncomfortable in your new choices was normal. That the brain was going to do everything it could to sabotage me.

All you need to do is keep going, because if you look back, your brain will want to go back to what it knows best, so that it doesn't feel squirmy and uncomfortable.

One thing that seemed to help was, rather than focusing

on what could go wrong, I could start thinking about what I wanted to come out of it. I wanted to come back to England with a firmer sense of what I wanted and needed from life. However messy it got, that was the goal. I also wanted to see if this pressure I felt existed in other places, or whether it was a London thing.

I wanted to see whether I was placing limitations on myself, or whether it was a product of my environment.

Srini Pillay spoke about the illusion of freedom – which is where we tell ourselves that we could be free *if only* we made different choices. But what we don't account for is the fact that we create our own prisons because we are scared by the idea of freedom and its unpredictability.

Just before I left, I picked up some freelance work with my old company, and, by serendipity, I found myself chatting to Puja McClymont, a life coach, for a feature about flexible working. We just happened to be talking about different perspectives, and inspiration struck: 'Do you think the whole quitting-your-job-to-go-travelling thing is a myth and that the answers are closer to home?' I asked without going into detail or that I was asking for myself. 'Do people actually learn something from it?'

She paused and said, '[After travelling] ... you value life more. When you are working in an urban environment, everything is taken for granted and you are working pay cheque to pay cheque. You go into this monetary focus rather than a lifestyle focus. And you lose perception and a grasp of what is real, and what your values are.

'I've been in situations where I've asked clients what they value most in the world and they struggle. And those answers – whether it's family, a hobby, good health – they should come naturally. If people are challenged by that question, it's because they are doing for doing's sake.

'Remove yourself from that environment, and I think you will live a better life when you come back.'

Either way, in a few days, I was going to be in Bangalore, a city I called my second home, and my life in London as I knew it, for a time, was over.

I was going to try to experience everything with an open heart and mind.

~

'You should get her married off to someone,' my mother's friend Jamal tells her when I'm not in earshot, on a pleasantly warm October evening in Bangalore.

It's only been two days since I left England for my three-month stint in India, but already Jamal is messing with my Om Shanti Om, let's-be-a-dandelion-in-the-wind ethos.

Mum passes the information on to me after he has left, when she's certain he's too far away for me to go hunt him down with a baseball bat.

I don't think Jamal is a terrible person, but there are so many things I want to say to this man – to educate him, ask him questions – but I am already defeated by the time I reach halfway into my argument.

A person like this is always going to think a man is my

solution. A person like this, who doesn't live any kind of life I want, doesn't deserve the arrangement of my words or a chastisement.

What does he know of the love in my life after Rob left it? Does he know that this trip with my parents is a form of love, a commitment we are making to each other to create memories, to learn more about each other?

Before I met Rob, I thought that a romantic love was the most important love of all. We prioritise it over every other type of love. I suppose it's because, on a primal level, in heterosexual relationships, a union of that type is a means to an end: to have kids.

I also felt it was a right. Pre-Rob, I firmly believed that everyone had a someone waiting out there for them, the right sock to their left one, the other turtle dove, the perfect match. I also heavily believed in fate and destiny, and I visited people who read tarot cards and coffee grounds who assured me this would happen.

(All of this stuff, by the way, was placed in a psychological bin and torched with a flamethrower after Rob died.)

When I met Rob, I thought that this was the universe finally paying up. Most people who go through trauma go Full God or discover some sort of genuine spirituality or, like me, realise there is no fucking rhyme or reason to the universe – bad things happen, good things happen, the end.

What this means in a post-Rob world is that I've come to realise that our lives are built upon a shore of so many different types of love. Maybe I didn't quite appreciate them all before, my family and friends. Maybe I took a lot of them for granted. But when that tsunami came and washed me out to sea, they were there, waiting for me to return to them.

They made me laugh, they made me food. They pressed cards into my hands, sent flowers. They let me rage, they let me cry. They didn't always get it right, but they never gave up trying.

I know that I can't change the mindset of aeons, that people will not believe I am truly healed from Rob's death until I find myself in a serious, romantic relationship. But there's a quietness in me that wants to honour all these other loves.

Spending time with Mum and Dad was a huge part of that. I remember Mum saying, after her own mother passed away, that she wished she had asked more questions, spent more time with her.

I didn't want that to happen with them. I wanted to know about them as adults to better understand them, and our family.

Because especially when it comes to parents, there is a terrible truth about your lives together. Most of us have never known what it's like to not have them around. Whether they drive you up the wall, whether you spend more time avoiding them than you do spending time with them, whether you love hanging out with them – whatever the size and shape of your relationship, we can't imagine them not being there because they have never *not* been there.

The sound of their voices and the scent of them are pressed into the tiniest, biggest, most formative of memories. And what do you do with such a thing, that has existed in your life for ever? You assume it's going to be around for ever.

Call it the glimpse backstage, but the truth of our relationship is that at least one of us is not going to make it beyond a certain point in time. It's uncomfortable thinking: our brains hate it; our hearts despise it.

So for someone to say that I needed to get married in order to experience love in my life – just, no. I had love in my life. It wasn't that I was turning my back on romantic love, but I wanted to make an active choice in my relationship with my parents, while they were still here, to prioritise and nurture this love a little.

There was this unassuming moment one day in their back garden in England. We were sitting in the sun, and Mum was chattering away, her gardening gloves flung on the table, secateurs shiny with the ooze of newly cut stems. I memorised every part of her: her short, curly hair, her pretty face with her tiny nose and eyes fizzing with energy, her brown skin freckled with sun spots, the sound of her voice.

Dad, so much taller than her, came through the patio door, in his slow lope of a walk, carrying three glasses and a bottle of prosecco. I took in his moustache, which he has always had, his rounder nose, his strong arms (despite being in his seventies because he's a fitness nut), and I wanted to breathe them both in and make that moment last for ever.

I know they have never pressured me, but I also know it would make them happy if I settled down with someone. It would mean, maybe, that I hadn't lost the rest of my life to the loss of Rob, as much as they loved him.

But I'm not ready to let go of this love yet. I am greedy with it; I want an endless afternoon of prosecco, of watching weird daytime-films-based-on-a-true-story with Mum, coffees in the gym with Dad. I know it's selfish, but I don't want to let go of them yet.

'Married off,' Jamal says? He probably doesn't have much love in his life.

The emotion of it sits hunched in my shoulders, while we all try to shake off our lives in England.

Mum and Dad are retired, and they spend almost half of their year in India to escape from the British weather, and to spend time with their siblings and friends who are mostly based here.

I have my own life in Bangalore; I spent several of my most formative years here. They have a sweet little modern flat in the centre of town, where the old Christian quarter used to be. It's a short Uber to the main shopping malls and the park I like to run in. I still keep in touch with my old school friends, the ones I made when I was here from the ages of seven and twelve, and although our lives are so different, they all contain that spark I love in my friends: funny, clever women.

When we were growing up, Bangalore was a leafy, green sprawl that never got too hot, or too cold, and the arteries of the city ran with veins of chlorophyll and oxygen. Now, gasoline, steel and glass have carved up the roads, but there is still beauty to be had in it. Rain trees spread their quiet, magnificent arms across roads packed with traffic, gulmohars with flowers as red as flame. Palm trees, coconut trees, bamboos creating dramatic archways and carefully tended gardens are found in quiet, little nooks.

I keep coming back here because there are deeper associations to love and fulfilment and belonging, fused to a primordial signature in my brain of what Bangalore is. The smell of rain, the whispering border where a light breeze carried over the hilltops meets skin sticky with humidity from the lick of sea. The sight of stone temples and their fresh, plump flowers; jasmine before the day has pressed them into a brown mess, bright marigolds puffing themselves against the day's heat.

Like most Indian cities, the older parts are a chaotic tangle of streets. The roads can get dusty, the buzz of motorbikes and scooters mingles with the roar of trucks and imported BMWs. Here is where the best architecture is, or what remains of it. Tiny colonial gems with sprawling gardens and cooling verandas, ancient shopfronts with lattice work, old private members' clubs. The wider, cleaner streets and big, glossy malls tend to be a bit further out.

People back in England ask me about Bangalore and I say, 'Don't bother coming here, honestly.'

They look surprised, but there isn't anything for a tourist here. My frequent visits (almost yearly) are based on the memory of the Bangalore I used to know, not the one it is now. There is nothing really here to surprise me; it's more like a second skin that I put on now and then.

In my parents' flat, the spare room has a balcony. Usually on my first morning I sit on it and see the tree that is home to a bunch of fruit bats. We only know that because of nature nerd Rob who discovered them. He loved it here and used to smoke cigarettes on this exact spot. I look down the length of the street, the big, open recreational ground to the left, the tiny Ganesh temple behind the apartment block. At the end of the road sits a guy wearing a *lungi* who irons clothes; further down is the man who collects paper and sells it on.

My aunts and uncles drift through the flat over the next few days. Sometimes they call me by the nickname of my younger years, Poorni, a word that unlocks a chest filled with memories I haven't thought about for so long. I'm the second-youngest of the cousins, so one of the babies of the family. It is hard, I think, for them to reconcile that I am thirty-seven, a fully grown woman who has an entire career and life back in England.

As these thoughts sleet through, I increasingly have to keep my doubts in check: *Hang on, I no longer have those things, so what defines me here?*

A big part of unpicking expectations is to understand where we come from better. What drives us? Where do we feel the pressure coming from? Why do we want the things we do, and does that need come from ourselves or someone else?

I already knew about the set of expectations I felt living in London, and subsequently the ones I had of myself.

But what did it mean in the bigger sense, taking into account my Indian self?

It's a running joke that if you are from the Indian sub-continent and you aren't married with kids, it doesn't matter if you're the prime minister. Your community doesn't care about your ability to make millions or wield lots of power if you haven't walked down a marriage aisle.

Where does it place someone like me? In other parts of India, widows are viewed as bad luck; they can be shunned and abused. They even have dietary restrictions put upon them, such as only being allowed to eat one meal a day or having to go vegetarian. They most certainly do not go on Tinder and eat cocktail sausages.

While we joke about it, there is a certain darkness to this rigidity we have around markers for success. It's not unique to India – Middle Eastern and Far East Asian cultures have similar drivers: get good grades, get married, have kids, honour your family.

The darkness comes because it doesn't create a lot of give for people who may be capable of some or none of those things. Where does it place South Asian people who struggle with mental health? Mental illness is still poorly understood, and people think it's all in the mind, and that, if you really wanted to, you could get better by thinking your way out of it. I've heard people who are doctors, and should know better, profess this belief despite all evidence to the contrary.

In some cases it is ignored; it is certainly not widely talked about. When a person exhibits behaviour due to their mental illness, it is not understood or examined. Mental pain is not acknowledged or treated with kindness; it is mostly viewed as weakness, or it's that person's fault. So a lot of mental illness remains hidden, self-medicated and misunderstood.

It has struck me as the great paradox: that Indians by and large disbelieve in something like mental illness, yet have a huge capacity for belief in faith, superstition, witchcraft and spiritualism.

On the one hand, it's impossible for people to think someone could be made ill by their own brain; but on the other, it's totally reasonable that Mr Gupta shagged Mrs Reddy because black magic compelled him to.

Belief rolls through the streets like an invisible fog. It has made countless entries into literature and song. It is so powerful that some people who have been educated in the best universities will consult their numerologist after looking at the Dow.

No wonder Elizabeth Gilbert found it so inspirational; belief in the unknown and divine liberates you from the randomness of the world. It places sense where senseless things have happened.

My parents and I arrive in the midst of one of India's biggest religious festivals, Navarathri.

On our way to dinner to celebrate their wedding anniversary, we see people out and about, some clutching jasmine, others lighting incense in roadside shrines – moving through ritual after ritual for the impending holiday.

In between slapping our legs to ward off mosquitoes, my dad tells me about this man – 'the rolling sadhu' – who rolled on the ground for 4,000 miles as part of a religious penance. 'He became ill, dirty water fell into his mouth, but he didn't give up,' my dad said.

We all think about this for a moment.

'So what do you think?' he says.

I wonder about the effort of will and belief that would compel someone to roll on a dog-poo, cow-poo, human-poo, shattered-glass, spittle-flecked floor for 4,000 miles.

Maybe this is something to be congratulated and a sign of God's will, but I say, 'Look, Dad, you couldn't pay me to roll to the *restaurant*, and Google Maps says it's only ten minutes away.'

He then tells me about this other man in Bangalore, who used to be Muslim but converted to Hinduism. 'Is that possible?' I interrupt. 'I thought you couldn't convert.'

Anyway, my dad says, shaking my question off, this guy had managed to reinvent himself into some sort of local guru. He managed to gather a small but fiercely loyal following and, a few years ago, they all embarked on a journey to travel by foot from the southernmost tip of India to the northernmost tip.

It took them eighteen months.

'EIGHTEEN MONTHS!' Dad exclaims. We all sit in silence for a moment taking this information in.

I can't persuade my friends to join me on a walking holiday for eight hours, I think, let alone eighteen months.

'I wonder,' he says thoughtfully, 'what emptiness these people have, and what they, in turn, see in this man that he fills it.'

His words are so precise and poignant it makes me remember something about my dad. We all know Dad the doctor, and his tales of A&E – from the guy who got a vacuum cleaner nozzle stuck up his bum to the woman who thought she was ill because she had blue discolouration around her wrists and neck (it was clothing dye).

But I'd forgotten that, beyond being the reassuring, moustachioed father figure in my life, beyond helping me move house from random flat-shares, beyond being the breadwinner, there is Dad the poet. He used to write poetry before he got married – reams and reams of it. In the dark car, his words hang in the air, glimmering like spun gold as we speed on to our destination.

~

We don't really know our parents or grandparents as people. Not in the same way we do our friends, partners or colleagues.

We have this idea of them that was set back when we were kids, and because a lot of us don't ask many questions of our older folk, there are basic things about them we don't know. Often, these are surprising things – acts of innovation, self-belief, independence.

They can inspire and teach us a lot about our lives, but the problem is we don't ask the questions, and by the time that generation reaches a certain age, all of the boldness of their youth gets distilled into concern around how you're living your life. We don't initiate conversations because we don't want to be nagged, but it means we're also missing out on a lot.

My parents are immigrants, and I remember when I first started asking them questions about their lives. Gone were Mum and Dad, who toiled all day at work, lectured me about saving my pennies and spent weekends watching *Strictly Come Dancing* with a glass of wine. Here were Jaya and Ashok, whose stories are those laced with the hard-won gloss of pioneers.

There are stories of a thoroughbred white horse named Ruksh, forbidden loves, schools set in Ghana and Ethiopia, weightlifting competitions, terrible tales involving beetroot, a young girl fighting for her life, and a young boy bunking off school smoking cigarettes.

Mum and Dad may seem like they live a comfortable life now, holidaying and having fun, but their origins stories inspire me.

Mum was a sickly child born to Nagaveni and KK Shetty, child number three of five children. It turned out she had a hole in the heart and was not expected to live very long. But every year she kept going until she made it to the age of nineteen, when she met the man who changed her life – or, rather, saved her life. It was a man named Dr Hegde, who was staying with them as a boarder while he studied for his exams. He suggested to her parents that she have heart surgery. It was relatively new surgery in those days.

She packed her little suitcase and admitted herself to hospital. ON HER OWN, PEOPLE. FOR <u>OPEN HEART SURGERY</u>. The rest of the family visited her once the surgery was done, and slowly she recovered. Before the surgery, she was told she may not live to forty, and definitely wouldn't be able to have children.

She survived, and it was the making of her. She went on to get married, have Priya and myself, find herself her own career and build a life from scratch. She went to work in London and still cooked dinner every night. Currently, she's sixty-seven, and she lifts heavier weights in the gym than most women half her age.

Dad had a different upbringing. He was one of four and the baby of his family.

There is only one picture I have seen of him without his moustache – he looks young, too young to belong to us, but I suppose he didn't at that time. Gawky, long legs and round, solemn eyes that belie a cheekiness for cadging cigarettes and stealing his brother's scooter.

When he was sixteen, his father unexpectedly passed away at the age of forty-nine, in their little blue house that was our first proper home when we moved to Bangalore.

Although he wanted to go into agriculture, they rejected him because he had a stammer. He then applied to medical school, and the person who interviewed him took him to the head of the school for a second opinion.

'Will his stammer get in the way?' the interviewer asked the head. 'I don't see why it should impede his ability to be a doctor,' he replied, and they accepted him.

To this day, Priya and I instantly soften around other people who have a stammer. I cried when I watched *The King's Speech*. It's our love for Dad that flows through, built on everything he had to do to overcome it, and what he made of himself in spite of it.

Dad went on to become an orthopaedic surgeon and he has helped countless people, including myself. I credit him with saving my life because he picked up on a heart murmur I had in my early thirties and forced me to go to the hospital for a check-up.

It turned out that I too had a hole in the heart, but unlike Mum it wasn't evident from birth and I'd managed to keep going until I started to develop symptoms of breathlessness. If it had gone undetected I could've had a stroke or a heart attack.

By his own admission he was hugely under-confident as a kid, but he found refuge in fitness via the piddly weights section at his university gym. 'The maximum weight', he said, 'was a 12kg dumbbell.'

'Dumbbell singular?' I asked. He nodded. Fitness as therapy and confidence-boosting is something we have in common. When Rob passed away, fitness was what I found comfort in, when being around people got too much.

At the age of seventy-one, he still goes to the gym six times a week, and, last I heard, he was signing up to cycle London to Brighton.

I wish I could've seen a picture of him when he was a medical student, taking part in the Gulbarga Medical College Bodybuilding Competition at university. It was a story I told all of my friends at school after some relative told me my dad was a champion weightlifter and came first. 'HE WON,' I crowed. 'My dad can kick your dad's ASS.'

Then, after years of telling this story, I recently found out he came third. 'Hang on,' I said, 'how many people took part?'

'Four,' he replied, and went back to making his coffee. 'What?' he said when I looked at him, shocked, as if our entire father–daughter relationship had been a lie.

Ashok and Jaya are inspiring in that they have taught me about resilience and strength, but the stories of *their* parents are truly exceptional.

I learned more about them as we left Bangalore and journeyed to Assam, a place known for its tea but not known for tourism. Few of us have ventured to the little-trod northeast of India unless you work in the military or air force, like my uncle Ajit did.

Most people said, 'Why the hell are you going to Assam?'

We were going to Assam because it was a place Mum and I were both interested in visiting. We'd been to Goa and Kerala dozens of times, and this part of India was shrouded in mountains, mist and the unknown. I was drawn to its secrecy.

After we land in its main city, Guwahati, I'm concerned this is just like any other part of populated India. A smattering of the rich among the swarm of the poor, interesting signboards such as 'Fooding and Lodging', mini eruptions of garbage and cows sauntering across lanes of traffic with their standard 'fuck you' attitude.

But after a few hours, Guwahati gives way to the more remote road leading to the Kaziranga national park. It has only just opened after the monsoon, and people are scarce on the road. After settling in, early next morning we decide to take a guide and a Jeep to do a little exploring.

If Guwahati was a clenched fist of smells and smog, Kaziranga is the undulating back; broad, open plains and wetlands and tall green grasses petering into pools of rainwater. In the morning, she looks wild, vast and empty, like a beautiful woman roused from a deep sleep.

Clouds gather low at the line of dark hills in the distance, as a steady pink glow rolls across the earth, capturing the sun's yawning reflection in the still, blue water.

The reason we are here is because it's the one place you can get very close to rhinos. Unlike elephants, who like the nuzzle and comfort of a herd, rhinos don't like anyone near them, least of which, other rhinos.

Suddenly we see one – a leathery Moses that looks as if it's standing on a lake of water. Somewhere beneath its toes must be a hidden bank of earth.

As the Jeep picks up speed again, I ask my parents if my grandparents ever came to Assam.

No, Mum says. They did much bigger things. In 1956, less than ten years after independence, her father, KK Shetty, decided to apply for a job in Ethiopia. He had never been to Africa, and back then there was no Instagram, no hashtag vacay, no way of knowing about a place unless you read a book or someone you knew had been there.

The reason he applied was because he perceived he was turned down for a job in India due to the rigged nature of the caste system. The job he wanted went to a Brahmin – a higher caste than him – who was less qualified.

Three years after the entire family moved to Ethiopia, my grandfather discovered an injustice regarding pay.

'He found out that the pay for teachers doing the same job was based on where they came from,' says Mum. 'Americans got top pay, then English and so on, and the Indians were one up from the bottom, which was the Ethiopians!

'He had fought for independence and equality and was not prepared to be insulted, and so when a job came up in Ghana – which had also just gained its independence – we all went there.'

They stayed in Ghana for six years, and during that period they went twice to Europe as a family, and once to the United States as a couple alone.

I can't imagine the scale of ambition, first for my grandfather KK to move to a continent he had never been to before, and then to amplify that ambition by taking themselves and their kids to places other immigrants could only dream of at that time.

I marvel at the bravery, and I think of all these incredible parents and grandparents who are hidden away in plain sight.

Grandparents may not seem incredible, at first. They may be camouflaged with cardigans and comfy chairs, they may ask you the same question an insane amount of times and have a wonky knee that always dominates talking points, but like a diamond covered in soot, dust off your apathy, spend some time with them and you may just find stories that will help guide you and give you the courage to do what you really want to.

My grandmother on my father's side was called Parvathy. We share the same nose and face shape. She was a firecracker of a woman: beautiful, with a signature look of red lipstick, glossy black hair and big sunglasses. My father's father was called Babu, and there is no one who doesn't describe him as a truly moral man. He worked high up in local government as the Commissioner of the Corporation of Bangalore, and was known for being scrupulously honest. He and KK were in fact friends, and he was so clever and won so many book prizes for academic excellence that KK had to help him carry the books home.

Although he was quiet and solid, and my grandmother Parvathy was the sparkler at any party, they complemented each other perfectly. It also makes me aware that, for most of my life, I've also chosen quiet men – men who are completely different when it's just me and them, but who in a crowded room veer on being solemn.

'To us he was serious and quiet,' my dad said, 'but he accomplished a lot academically and had immense moral fibre. But he also had a dry sense of humour. I remember my mum had a gold chain and it had these mangoes hanging off it. One day, one of the mangoes fell off and he said: "I think it got too ripe."'

Dad laughs, his eyes crinkling at the memory.

On Mum's side, Nagaveni, my maternal grandmother, was a miracle baby. Her mother didn't have her until she was a lot older, at the age of forty, and because she was her parents' only child and her father was so paranoid about something happening to her, he wouldn't let her take swimming lessons. 'If you want to swim,' he said, 'swim on the bed.' A confused Nagaveni tried paddling in a swell of sheets and gave up.

By the time she met KK, her parents had passed away, and KK was busy working as a teacher and being part of the Gandhian freedom movement against Britain's colonial rule (he went to jail for cutting a telegraph wire). They met at night school, where he was teaching.

'Wait,' I interrupt my mother in the middle of telling this story, 'she was his STUDENT!!!!'

Apparently, Nagaveni wasn't a coy, impressionable little flower. 'She was his most difficult student,' Mum says, 'always giving him trouble. But that's what he liked about her.'

Even the Jeep driver has pricked up his ears.

'Well,' says Dad, 'that's also how my dad met my mother.'

'WHAT!' Mum and I both yell.

'Yes,' says Dad, 'he was her teacher.'

'Was it night school?' Mum asks. Dad says he thinks it was.

If the driver wasn't paying attention before, he definitely is now.

While Mum and I are still reeling at the news that our entire bloodline is based on the success rate of teacher–student relationships, Dad tells us that, actually, his father's family didn't want him to marry his mother, Parvathy.

'But why?' I ask. 'She was a total babe.'

The reasons are lost with the ashes of my grandparents, unfortunately, but what follows next is like something from a film script. Despite being from the same caste, Babu's family disapproved. A secret meeting was arranged for him to meet Parvathy's family, but on the day, his family caught wind of what was going to unfold.

To prevent him from going to meet her, they locked him in what was known as the 'bootha room', which a lot of bigger family houses had. Bootha in our language means 'spirit', and it's a room set aside for the spirits of our ancestors. Generally it's considered to be the spookiest room in the house, so presumably they were trying to make him scared. 'And I don't think it helped that there were actual bats flying around,' says Dad.

Babu decided a bootha room was not going to stop him seeing the woman he loved. So what did he do? He escaped through the roof. Then they married, without his parents' blessing.

Nagaveni and KK weren't allowed to be together either because they were from different castes.

Their only wedding guests in 1947 were KK's sister Radha and her husband, who had also been shunned for marrying out of caste. I'd only ever known these people when they were much older, and I wish I had known about this fire, this effort of will they had once possessed to do what they wanted for love, even if it meant no one accepted it.

Apart from all that, two things stand out in my mind about my grandmothers.

Parvathy managed to put four kids – one fighter pilot, three doctors – through school after Babu died, and she did so with her intelligence, wit and tenacity. It was no mean feat in the 1960s as a single Indian woman. When we were growing up, I knew she had been widowed young but I never stopped to think what that must have been like for her. Now that I know from personal experience, there is only admiration.

The second was that Nagaveni used to go to the hospital to give birth on her own because, back then, childbirth wasn't really a big deal. Forget the husband coming with you and an overnight bag – when she felt her contractions, she'd take her bag, stop at a local café she liked on the way, have her meal and then went on to have her child.

When I knew her, she was already old, and I was one of

the youngest grandchildren. I just knew her as the grandma who was lovely to us and made an amazing chicken curry but who wouldn't let us watch *Thriller* because she thought it was too scary for our tiny child brains. Who knew that she carried all of this strength, all of these stories around with her? I certainly didn't.

Our guide signals us to be quiet – he's spotted a rhino with her baby and they are so close I can see the pockmarks on her hide. The baby's tail is waggling as it feeds hungrily from its mother, mud washing over both of them as they move around in the water to keep cool.

We move on to give the rhinos some space, and our path cuts to the wide, open plains again.

India uncurls east like an arm outstretched, and in her palm are lagoons of green, and broad, open skies that echo only with the flutter of birds.

She's known for being hectic, high-maintenance with her traffic, teeming with too many people. But like the humans who live on her surface, she's not any one thing; she has so many different faces.

Now she turns to me, and her eyes are lake water and her lips red earth.

I carry all of this new knowledge with me, these stories of unconventional beginnings.

My grandparents and parents had far fewer choices than I do, yet they made bold, brave choices.

KK moved his entire family to Africa, and this was a time before email, Facebook and WhatsApp. They kept in touch mainly by letters. Phone calls were a rarity and placed through the operator, and telegrams were greeted with fear because they were expensive and usually represented bad, urgent news.

It turns out even my great-grandmother didn't give up on the idea of having children, considering how late she had Nagaveni.

When we get back to Guwahati, it's the birthday of Gandhi, which means no alcohol is sold anywhere. Our hotel is perfectly adequate, but it's one of many crammed on a busy stretch of road near an open sewer, and mine is a room with a view. Of the sewer.

So we all take ourselves off to a boat ride along the mighty Brahmaputra, one of India's most famous rivers. It's called mighty because it is a beast of a thing, born in the crystal-clear waters of Tibet from the Chemayungdung glacier, and is just under 4,000km long. It runs through the Kailash range of mountains – the birthplace of the Hindu god Shiva the Destroyer – and its delta is home to 130 million people.

When it floods at the right level, it brings moisture and minerals to crops, provides fish for people to eat. But when it spirals out of control, it is called the Sorrow of Assam because of the high numbers of people it kills.

On the day of Gandhi's birthday, it's not flooding. The waters are remarkably calm after a long and trying monsoon, and the sun has chosen garments of lilac and peach as it makes an exit.

Boats are always pot luck in India – you never know if you're going to get something decent or a rust bucket two screws shy of sinking into the water. But our boat is surprisingly comfortable – there's even a menu for fried chicken drumsticks and puffy potato bhajis.

Towards the back of the boat is a small stage and a Casio keyboard decorated in flashing lights and plastic flowers. Karaoke?

No, it turns out. A middle-aged musician with skin the colour of dark chocolate eases into the chair, his pot belly just about fitting under the keyboard. He coughs, plinks on the keys a couple of times, and then starts singing Bengali love songs.

To pass the time, and because I'm curious, I ask Mum and Dad how they first met. 'Well,' says Mum, 'that story begins a bit before our first meeting.'

At the time, Mum was living with her parents in England. They had left Ghana because of the coup d'état that deposed Kwame Nkrumah, and sailed in one of the original migrant boats to England for their education.

Mum started working for a fruit and veg exporter in Spitalfields, and during that time, Parvathy had come over for a visit to see KK and Nagaveni. Mum was a bold little firecracker even back then, so she'd act as the official tour guide for visitors. She offered to take Parvathy out. They hit it off – 'because we were so similar,' Mum says – and in the camera department of Selfridges, Parvathy revealed that she would have loved to have Mum as her daughter-in-law.

'I asked her, as a joke, whether she had a son lurking under the bed. She said she had a son in medical school who she would like to marry me. I thought she was joking and didn't really say anything further at the time.'

But Parvathy wasn't joking, and a few months later, she brought up the topic with Mum's parents. It was then agreed that Mum would meet Dad when she was over in Bangalore visiting her sister Meera, who was pregnant at the time.

I ask Mum whether she had dated anyone before or whether she always knew she'd have an arranged marriage, and she looks thoughtful. 'We were raised mostly in Ethiopia and Ghana, so I didn't really have much of an opportunity to make friends, let alone meet boys, because most of our classmates were often ten to fifteen years older than us due to the inequality of education over there. So I suppose I did always think I'd have an arranged marriage.

'The only exception was when I went to college and met a really nice chap named Lawrence. He asked me to marry him but I panicked and said no.'

Dad hoots with laughter, so I swivel my attention to him. I knew Dad was in a long-term relationship before he met Mum, so he didn't always believe he'd have an arranged marriage. 'So what did you think when you met Mum for the first time?' I asked. Ever the economical wordsmith, he said, 'I thought, okay, she looked nice.'

I try to imagine being a fly on the wall of the first meeting of Ashok and Jaya Shetty, but all I can imagine is Dad in bell-bottoms being extremely shy, and Mum with that 1,000 kilowatt smile. Above all, I can't even imagine how awkward it must have been. Or maybe it wasn't – maybe I'm just projecting how awkward I'd feel in such a situation.

'Alright then,' I ask Mum, 'what did you think of Dad when you first met him?'

She looks shifty. 'Well, he seemed shy but I really liked that he didn't try to impress me by boasting, and when he spoke or asked a question, it was something he genuinely wanted to know the answer to.'

'And?'

'And … okay, I wasn't bowled over at first – he had this Mexican-style moustache and oil on his hair,' she admits, 'but he did have a good figure.'

Once the marriage was arranged, Mum had to go back to England, but flew back a few weeks before the wedding.

Even though it was an arranged marriage, and they didn't know each other very well, it was clear from the smallest of gestures that they both wanted and believed in a life of romance.

'When I went for the wedding,' Mum says, 'Dad would come and see me every day.' In classic Dad mode, he wouldn't say much, but a few days before the wedding, Mum says, 'He asked me to go for a walk with him in the night and he held my hand for the first time – so sweet. Just like Hollywood!'

We all burst out laughing. 'Or more like Bollywood,' she cackled.

'But hang on,' I say. 'When did you arrange to go to England?'

My grandparents KK and Nagaveni had moved to England from Ghana in the 1960s when there were no visa restrictions, and, as their child, Mum had indefinite leave to stay. One of the conditions of the marriage was that Dad would move over and settle with Mum in England.

Shortly after their wedding in September 1974, they were then apart for six months, while Dad started the process to get his visa. 'SIX MONTHS!' I exclaim to Mum and Dad. When Rob and I got married, I couldn't have imagined being apart from him for six *weeks*, let alone half a year.

'But, Poorna,' Mum says, 'we didn't even question such things, in the way you'd question it now. We didn't even really think for ourselves – our parents did that for us. We just did what was expected.'

As each generation grows and evolves, they move one step further from the expectations laid out for them by their parents. But we never evolve beyond a set of expectations – they simply change shape. Present day, most people in the Western world aren't expected to marry for political or economic reasons, as they once were. Men aren't expected to be economically responsible for their families in the same way. Women aren't expected to stay at home and look after the children.

But those expectations still persist on some level, and endeavour to shape our lives.

Mum and Dad may have done what was expected, but

they also evolved their own way of dealing with the consequences of those decisions.

While apart, Dad wrote her letters, and they kept the tiny flicker of that flame alive, that began between two people who barely knew each other but wanted to build a life together.

Eventually, he came over and started studying for his Fellowship of the Royal Colleges of Surgeons (FRCS), the qualification for senior surgeons. I marvel at how many threads pulled together to enable them to marry, for Priya and I to be born, and for Leela to come into this world to carry on our stories and our lives.

By this time, night has fully settled in around the boat, and it's no longer possible to see down the length of the river as it stretches towards the Bay of Bengal.

Everyone's eyes swivel to the tiny stage where our musician is transitioning into 'party mode' as the tunes change to more upbeat Hindi songs.

'Good evening, ladies, gentlemen, boys and girls,' he says. 'I would like to invite you all to dance.' He gestures at the small area in front of his keyboard.

Everyone is excruciatingly sober because of the alcohol ban: it's unlikely anyone is going to take him up on his offer. He starts playing 'Ek, Do, Teen', a classic disco song from when I was a kid, and his stage lights start going crazy in time to the music. He even pops a pair of sunglasses on. *Lock up your daughters, folks . . .*

Still, no one gets up. Then Mum tugs at Dad's shirt.

'Come on, shall we dance?' she says. It'll be a cold day in hell before Dad dances without a beer in his hand. I'm the same. I couldn't fathom getting up in front of all those people.

When Mum realises Dad and I aren't going to move, she stands up. Where is she going? The toilet?

No, she's heading for the stage. I am blown away by this: Mum is going to dance, and she doesn't need a beer. She doesn't care that everyone is looking, or that she might feel silly – she just goes for it.

As she spins under the lights, she looks so beautiful, so free, you can almost see her spirit and energy curling and uncurling around her. It is the most magnificent thing I have ever seen. She's saying: *I want to dance and life is too damn short to worry about what other people think.*

I am so glad I got to witness this, got to see her living in the moment like the Roman candle she is. Slowly I see other people getting up to dance, encouraged by Mum's little act of bravery. I wonder what it must be like to be Dad, in love with a woman who, at times, lights everything she touches in this dazzling glow.

I always thought any bravery or rebelliousness I had was because I was emboldened by the freedom of the West.

Turns out it was in my blood the entire time.

6

SO THIS IS WHAT
CLOUDS TASTE LIKE

We hire a car to take us to the neighbouring state, Meghalaya. I remember reading about it as a child. Its name literally translates in Sanskrit to 'The Abode of Clouds', so it always seemed like an ethereal wonderland where castles floated in the air.

It was nicknamed by the British Raj as 'Scotland of the East', a name that still lurks around not because the Scottish are holding onto it, but because Indian journalists and Indian tourist boards still persist in using it.

Anytime it gets written about, it's referred to as Meghalaya, Scotland of the East, because of that lingering colonialist attitude that anything affiliated with the West increases its allure and value.

Meghalaya doesn't need the help.

It's not a fairy-tale confection of turrets peeping through the clouds as I imagined as a child, but it is arresting in its beauty. I have never seen anything like it in India, even when I visited the lower Himalayas.

At first, the view from our hotel is pretty enough. Below our feet, the land cuts away to a small valley, stretching in greenery to the water's edge; lanky trees and dense under-growth around the edges of a lake. Blue at its heart, with clouds draped across it like a white shawl, half-heartedly contemplating a future of rain.

Meghalaya is home to the rainiest place on earth; it's like a train station for clouds.

The next day I make the journey to do something I've always dreamed of: walk 6,000 steps down and up to see the double-decker root bridge in Cherrapunjee.

It used to be the wettest place on the planet, but appar-ently Mawsynram, 16km away, now holds that distinction. The people here devised a way of getting from one village to another during monsoon by coaxing living rubber trees into bridges.

The branches are teased into bamboo funnels and it takes about thirty to forty years to grow a bridge. There are about fifty single root bridges but only one double-decker – the top bridge was created after a period when the monsoon was so heavy, it flooded the first bridge.

Dad suggests coming, but this is something I want to do on my own.

I have long since felt that otherworldly places are where I feel Rob the most, and I won't be able to do that while having conversations about foot fungus and how much beer we'll need for the evening.

On the way there is a sign that reads:

Meghalaya: Where The Clouds Come To Romance.

The young guy I've hired as a driver, Susheel, is playing Justin Bieber, and it is entirely incongruous that this is the soundtrack to what greets me around the corner after we drive up the mountain.

'Ma'am,' he says plaintively, stopping the car.

I look up from my phone where I've been frantically trying to find music to drown out Bieber, and I see heaven.

Ahead of us is a large, long valley of mountains, each one tightly bound in a dense forest of green. Their shape and lines are moulded by folds of darkness, light teetering on the edge, fusing them together into a flowing river of rock.

They stretch into the distance, until at the very end is a mountain wreathed in mist and clouds. Above their peaks is the bluest sky, and crowning the scene is a blazing sun. The scene looks like every depiction of Eden in a Renaissance painting.

I get out and take a few photos, but there is nothing that can capture this. It is heart-lifting; it is heartbreaking. It perfectly captures the gladness of being alive and the sorrow that some people you love are no longer around to see it.

This is more than an arrangement of mountains, light and leaves – there is something else wound into this landscape. It is relief, it is comfort, it is the earth saying to me, *It will be okay.* You want everyone to see this, to feel this – your heart almost can't contain it.

We're ordered to get back in the car – some jobsworth with a clipboard is barking at Susheel to move on – and then, out of nowhere, we see a cloud heading towards us at the same level as our heads. I gasp as it rolls through me; I taste its dream of rain.

We start driving and then we are in a herd of clouds. Immediately the sky is gobbled up and everything around us is a ghost world. Beyond the outline of the nearest trees and a lone fence dissolving into motes of nothingness, this feels like what the afterlife should look like. There is no beginning and no end; we see a man's outline as he enters and disappears back into mist, curls of white following him as he leaves.

We sit quietly, feeling as if our existence in the present world is suspended for the time being. It is like floating.

When I think back to how I felt just after Rob died – not belonging to anyone, feeling no reason to stay in our world but neither compelled to follow him – this is that emotion sketched out in landscape.

~

One minute you are basking in the warmth and love of your parents, and the next, you are held in a field of clouds feeling like every atom in your body is coming apart at the seams.

A big reason for this journey is to figure some shit out, but another reason is also because I *don't* have anything to lose. 'You don't have dependants,' a friend said. I know they were being helpful, and they were right. But it also makes me think: *Jeez, I don't have any dependants.*

If something happens to Priya, or Mum and Dad,

they have another person to sound the alarm pretty soon after. I've been so headstrong and misanthropic at times – 'DON'T freak out if you call me and I don't answer the phone' – that in the event something does happen, I have no one to blame but myself. I mean what *do* I do if a fish bone gets stuck in my throat or I spoon so much peanut butter into my mouth I can't breathe?

I asked them not to pressure and nag me. I haven't so much as detached the umbilical cord, I've torched it and sent the ashes directly into the sun.

I had a dependant, and I lost him. I lost a 6ft 1 human who had blue eyes and calloused hands. A mallet thumb from an accident he'd had as a child. I lost Sunday lunches with him, choosing linen for our bed, discussions around holidays. I lost someone to bitch with at weddings, someone who made me feel lustful every day I was with him. I lost my best friend. I lost the biggest love I ever had.

I know why I didn't have dependants. Sure, dependants meant you had someone to nurture and love, but dependants were also people you could lose. When I thought about the idea of losing my niece Leela, my heart became so sharp in my chest I stopped breathing. Dependants? I barely survived losing Rob – losing anything more would finish me off.

But does that make me a coward? For all that I preach about living a full and ordered life, was I my own enemy by not allowing myself to have anything I could possibly lose? Yes, I had lost almost everything, but when I did have it all, I also fought for and protected it with a strength and capacity I didn't know I was capable of.

When Rob told me he was a heroin addict, I didn't feel a moment's hesitation about helping him and getting him well. A lot of people said, 'I'm impressed you stayed with him. I don't know that I would've been able to do the same.' When it came to his safety, I knew exactly what I had to do.

But when the idea of us separating became real, and I realised I'd have to work out what to do with my life without him, I thought, 'I don't know where to start.'

I thought about dividing our furniture, our art we bought on holidays, our kitchen utensils. Even the thought of who would take the pasta strainer undid me – I couldn't fathom having the energy to do it.

Of course, we didn't have to do it, in the end, because the end was so much worse than figuring out the inventory of our lives together.

Most of the time, I don't feel broken. But when other people sometimes look at me, I know their eyes are looking for the crack that tells them how and when I was smashed apart, and then put back together.

I know people are horrified on my behalf by my loss, and sometimes, when they are going through something tough, they'll say, 'I know it's nothing compared to what you went through.'

It's not comparable, I often say. It is impossible to use the currency of my story as an exchange rate as to how you should feel about your own life. Our hearts don't weigh the same, and we don't have identical histories.

But sometimes, when I wonder how on earth I am going to approach a sense of normality, or at least appearing normal, I come across a story of someone who has lost so much more. I'm not indulging in misery tourism, but I'll read about someone who lost multiple family members, or suffered a different but equally bad trauma immediately after one trauma.

One lady was Victoria Milligan, who was enjoying a day out on a speedboat with her husband and four children. They had an accident and the boat overturned with all of them in the water – the kill cord hadn't been attached, so they floated in the water as the boat came back round for them over and over again. In the end, she lost her husband and eight-year-old daughter, and she lost her left leg as it had been slashed beyond repair by the propellers.

Victoria wrote her personal account of this and her views on resilience when I worked at *HuffPost*. She said, 'I have had to adapt to a very different future to the one I thought I would have and one without two very precious people in it.

'Resilience is something we all need to learn in this increasingly uncertain world; the sooner we are able to get up again and dust ourselves off when something goes wrong, the better able we are to adapt to any new situation.'

I'm not saying that I'm looking at Victoria's life – or anyone who has experienced severe, multiple trauma – and am thinking, 'God, it could be so much worse.'

I'm saying that I look at Victoria's life, and I see the solidified version of the human spirit and its will to survive.

In the midst of all that death, I see hope. I see someone who has overcome remarkable odds and who has earned the right to interpret and experience the world as they want to. Above all, what I see is the hardening of a truth within myself: that it is impossible for other people to know what your heart wants, and what it is capable of.

I'm not always so magnanimous, though. When I heard that Lucy, the wife of Paul Kalanithi – the late surgeon who wrote the bestseller *When Breath Becomes Air* – met a fellow widower, John Duberstein, whose deceased spouse Nina Riggs also wrote a book about dying from cancer, there was a part of me that was seriously jealous.

Mainly because I struggle with wondering who could possibly love me, and not be put off by what I've been through.

Sometimes being in these places of otherness are the only times I feel weightless, unburdened by it all.

~

I started dating about fourteen months after Rob passed away. Not the beautiful Lucy-and-John kind, more the right-swipe dating app here-today-gone-tomorrow kind.

Work was busy but not overwhelming, and on the weekends I would sequester myself away from the real world in my writing cocoon.

But then I took a proper, serious step back into the real world.

'It's not that I *need* to start dating,' I said to my friend Martin. 'I *want* to go on a date.'

The truth was I was starting to yearn for men. Not because I wanted to get into a relationship. But I missed the physicality of them. The smell of woody cologne and fresh shampoo. The stretch and sinew on their arms, stubble on their face. The feeling of a much bigger arm wrapped around me.

Shortly after I wrote the chapter of Rob's death in my first book, I needed to do something, anything, that was different to sitting in my room and writing.

When I hesitantly told people I was dating, they sighed happily because it meant – to them – that my heart had thawed and I was ready to love again. I was ready to do no such thing – I just needed some action.

Dating in my thirties was very different from the previous two decades. A lot of this is shaped by what other people think, versus how you may actually feel about it.

In your teenage years, it's a free-for-all: there are no expectations and you make your choices based on what band a person likes, or whether they've gone for the 10-hole Doc Martens over the 8-hole. You have limitless time to make mistakes.

In your twenties, things start to get a bit more intense. You begin with all the gorgeous hedonism of your university years, have a freak-out mid-decade, then spend the latter half trying to find someone to settle down with because if you don't do it by the time you hit thirty, your nethers will instantly desiccate and you'll be alone for ever.

Then you turn thirty and you find the world is as it always was, and your genitals haven't dropped off. You still have wriggle room, however, even if it doesn't feel like it.

In your mid-thirties and beyond, the assumptions about what you must want from your dating life, whether you are a man or a woman, grow bigger and uglier.

People assume you must want to settle down. For women, there is the extra kicker that they start referring to your biological clock in conversation when it's none of their business.

A lot is said about women's health and fertility – in fact, in the dating world, there's an entrenched, sexist assumption that women must be gagging to have kids because of the baby clock.

'Men can have kids at any age,' said a male friend.

'Well, yes, they can,' I countered. 'But so can women. Maria del Carmen Bousada de Lara was sixty-six when she gave birth to twins. It's sexist to assume that fertility is a woman's problem. After a certain age, your sperm goes off like a cheese sandwich in the sun, just like our eggs do, pal.'

Considering the fact that men's sperm counts decrease significantly after the age of forty, and that, for men, the risk of miscarriage is much higher if they father children after forty-five, I wonder why men don't get the same barrage of questions.

What places me in a unique position to observe what's

going on is that people just don't know what the fuck to do with me. That's because, more or less, there are three main clumps to which single people my age belong.

Clump one is usually full of people who have been single for a long period of time, and want to meet a significant other so they can fulfil the ambition of getting married and having kids. Clump two is people who have come out of a divorce or long-term relationship; they may or may not have kids. Clump three is the least common – like an O-negative blood type – and is filled with people like me and Victoria Milligan – widows, widowers, people who have an unusual backstory for why they are single.

When you're re-entering the dating world after a long time, it can naturally be daunting. None of this is helped by hanging out with the clump one types. They are jaded around dating and understandably so.

For years, they've had to go to dinner parties, Christmases, weddings and endure the relentless slew of 'when is it your turn?' The screw tightens as the years pass, with elderly relatives trying to blackmail them with their mortality: 'I'd love to see you settled before I die.' Trust me when I say that when that person's life flashes before their eyes, your wedding photo is not going to make the final cut of their defining moments.

That's not even factoring in the actual experience of dating itself. There is so much conflicting advice, from the rules of texting to where to find a partner in the first place.

'Well, he's within the three-day rule,' Mal said when

we were talking about a guy I was interested in. This guy would almost never reply to a text on the same day, and would take exactly two days to respond. I was upset and wanted to know if I was justified in being upset.

The three-day rule is that it's fine for someone to take three days to respond to your text message, but more than three days and it means they definitely don't like you. According to this rule, this guy's behaviour was totally fine because it was within the margin, when it was actually totally mad.

'Really?' I said. 'Who made this rule?'

'What do you mean?'

'I mean who set this rule? Was it a study of more than 2,000 people, who were a mix of age-appropriate men and women, and they arrived at a mathematical formula that revealed three days was fine? Even though we now live in a day and age where people can send FREE MESSAGES on WhatsApp and there is no excuse for them to take three days to get back to you? Even though this cretin has read-receipts set up on his phone? Or was it a rule made up by a woman who wanted to make herself feel better about some bozo who took three days to text her back?'

Mal looked at me like I'd lost it. I think I had.

'I just think,' I said, wiping the rabid froth from my mouth, 'that if someone likes you, whether they are a man or a woman, they don't take a specific time frame to message you back. *That* actually requires more thought and effort than just replying to the text straight away.'

That was one thing I learned from being with Rob. It's not rocket science. When we first got together, I didn't worry about whether he'd reply, because he did. So I didn't angst about whether or not the text actually got delivered, or whether he was in a coal mine with no reception.

Married or coupled-up friends don't think you should sign up to a dating app, but similarly don't have a warehouse full of hot, eligible people either. You go on a lot of dates because someone told you it's a numbers game. No one tells you that if you go on a lot of dates, the likelihood is you will also have a lot of bad dates, and it feeds into the idea that dating is a negative experience.

Stepping back into that when you are a fragile baby bird from whatever experience you have had can be tough. Or – as I choose to see it – it can act as a whetstone and sharpen what you want from dating.

I had to be physically attracted to them from the start. This whole 'they've got a great personality' thing may work for long-term relationships, but it wasn't working for me.

There was going to be no flexibility around the texting thing. If I started to feel like it was too much work or like I was hassling a guy, they were out.

Whatever the interaction – casual dating or relationship – I had to feel good about myself.

There had to be some type of connection – sense of humour, intelligence, something. The world of Tinder can work sometimes, but there is undeniably a fast-food element to it where people just meet up to have sex. Some people would just say, 'Hey, so can I come over?' before we'd even met. It boggled the mind.

Also, as perverse as this sounds in the context of being with other people, being with Rob taught me so much about myself, and how a person should feel about any form of romantic interaction.

When I met him, I don't think I realised how fragile my self-esteem was. I didn't learn how to fortify my sense of self in my twenties; how to make better, smarter choices around men.

When we met, it says a lot that my default expectation was that he wouldn't call, would shy away from connection, or would reveal himself to be a complete freak. (I mean he was a bird freak, but that was a softer, more lovable attribute than this one guy who invited another girl along to our date.)

It was more than just loving him. He helped me to love myself. What he saw in me made me look more closely at what I had to offer, and who I was as a person. And when I came through the other side of his death, when I was here because I'd fought to be here, I thought, 'Hang on, am I going to waste this new life on someone who doesn't make me feel great?'

I debated this (and won) with a friend, who said, 'Well, you felt like that because you were in a relationship. Casual dating is brutal and it sucks.'

'Hang on,' I replied, 'so what you're saying is that respect, or being kind, is only the preserve of people in relationships? And that if you aren't committed to someone, then they have the right of way to treat you like shit?'

As far as I see it, being a decent human doesn't just extend to your significant other. It should extend to your parents, your friends, the person who makes you coffee or hands you a newspaper in the morning. It should definitely extend to someone you've exchanged bodily fluids with.

More than that, there's the sexist, default expectation (along with the fact that obviously every woman wants kids simply because she has a womb) that women ALWAYS want more than what men want from them.

I'm sorry, but no. Maybe it's because once upon a time women were dependent on men to choose them because marriage represented a financial and social alliance back then. Or maybe that's part of the conditioning, the age-old story that a man will come along and sweep you off your feet. Maybe it's because a woman is told – repeatedly – that her worth amounts to nothing if she can't tick the boxes of romantic fulfilment and domestic success.

But saying that the default of casual dating is bad conversely feeds into the idea that marriage is always great, or that long-term relationships are always good.

Both aspects have the potential for good, and the potential for bad. It's time we were honest about it.

I told Mum and Dad I had started dating because I thought it might make them happy.

We were in a crowded pub in Victoria, squashed in by the

after-work crowd. Dad had just bustled over with a bottle of prosecco and three glasses.

'So I've started dating again, but I need to warn you – it's nothing serious.'

Mum and Dad nodded cautiously. In hindsight, I have to give them credit for their style of parenting. During my teenage years leading up to this point, they have somehow always known not to overcrowd Priya and me, and let us arrive at things in our own time.

'His name is Jake, and he's an engineer. He trains for Ironman, and he's really clever. But I don't think I'm going to see him for much longer.'

'Okay,' said Mum slowly, 'that's good to hear, Poo. Why don't you want to see him again?'

'We don't have much in common, and to be honest, I'm getting a bit bored.' I watched their reaction. Dad was busying himself pouring the wine.

Then Mum said the words that made me love her for ever, if I didn't already love her for ever. 'It's fine,' she said waving her hand. 'You date this one, then you find another one and then date that one.'

At the time, it was nothing short of relief. That Mum understood it wasn't about me replacing Rob, and that as an independent woman I had options, was huge.

Fast-forward twelve months to me and Dad in the car in India after Assam, on the way to the gym, and I relate an anecdote to Dad about a date I had before leaving England. My hands get really calloused from lifting weights, and when I was moaning about the peeling skin, Dad had said, 'No one will notice, it doesn't matter.'

I reply, 'Yeah, but . . .' and then I stop myself, realising I'm about to tell him this anecdote about a guy I was seeing in England, and then it dawns on me that I have no way of explaining who this person is.

For a start, he's about eleven years younger than me. Will Dad disapprove?

Then I think, 'Hang on, men have been doing this shit since the beginning of time! They never get crap for dating younger women. In fact, they'd probably get a pat on the back and a cigar to celebrate!'

That's the other thing about thirty-something dating – everyone has an opinion on who you should be doing it with, how you should be doing it. Not too young, not too old, what job does he do, will he fit in with our social circles? We hang out as a group at best ONCE A YEAR, so I'm not making my romantic choices based on how they slot into my social scene or whether they are age-appropriate.

Fuck it, I think, and I tell Dad.

'There's this guy I've seen a couple of times, Dad, and he was holding my hand. And he says, really deadpan, 'You're really pretty and you have lovely skin, but your palm? Your palm has the texture of a dog's paw.'

Dad and I both burst out laughing.

A few days later Dad says, 'So what about Dog Paw? Does he have the potential to be serious?'

I sigh. 'Dog Paw is twenty-five, Dad.'

Dad's eyebrows shoot up but he doesn't say anything.

'He's a great guy,' I continue, 'but he's too young.'

I am hyper-aware that the more time goes on, the more people are waiting for my next significant other. I can regale them with all the dating stories I like, but that's what they are holding out for.

They want me to have someone so I can join the dinner parties again, be there for group gatherings, kids' birthday parties. Or maybe they just don't want me to be lonely.

I think they forget that I had all of that, and I still got lonely.

Or maybe they think that with Rob, I judged things badly, maybe I made a bad choice. Do I wish I had known more, that things had been done differently? Yes, a thousand times, I do. Were things at times impossibly hard because of him? Of course. Do I regret being with Rob? No, because it wasn't all tragic.

During my life with him, I experienced my most challenging times, and I had to muddle through it on my own. But at the same time, I experienced the most love I have ever received and given in my life. All of those good moments, from being bought bunches of daffodils to a soft, long kiss with Rob, were worth all of it.

When people read about him – he had depression, hid an addiction from his wife – they may wonder if he was worth it. He could be a horror at times but of course he was worth it.

People are not measured on the Scales of Anubis: good or

bad. We are wholly compiled of shades of grey. So instead of imagining my capacity to put up with tough times, imagine instead the good he had in him, and how that was able to inspire that kind of love in a flinty-hearted woman.

There's another thought that still hangs in the air, unspoken, gathering molecules of emotion: what would her life have been like if she had met someone other than Rob?

Truly, I don't know. On the one hand, we had this huge, big love, and Rob told me early on that he had depression. He did everything right in one sense: added me to his pension because I was reckless about my own future, owned his own house, looked after me (mostly), was kind, considerate and funny.

Yet, I missed all the signs that he was a drug addict because I trusted him, and there was nothing in my brain that would connect those dots. That trust allowed him to manipulate me around his addiction, allowed things to spiral out of control, and he ended up virtually bankrupt. Genuinely, I thought that as long as you had love, you could do anything.

In the most brutal sense, the ending of every relationship should teach you something valuable and useful that you take into your next relationship. The biggest lesson for me was to ask more questions.

To push more, not allow the other person's sense of ego or pride to prevent me from finding out more about what I know in my gut isn't right. Rob was always vague about his schooling, distant about relationships he'd had when he was younger. That absolutely should've been something I asked more questions about.

Because really, it wasn't just about being a good partner, or figuring out how to better help Rob. I thought it was all about him for years because that's what being a carer does to you.

It was: what am I doing that nurtures and protects *me* as a person? Am I doing right by myself in being in this relationship that, yes, makes me happy on some days, but on other days makes me anxious, upset, bereft and lonely?

To survive Rob's death, I had to conduct an open dialogue between two halves of myself – the one that wanted to self-destruct and the one that wanted to live.

There's a saying that after the death of a child, parent or spouse, in order to get through the chaos and grief, you have to create a new normal. I don't really like the word 'normal', but I know the person I am is no longer the person I was when Rob was alive.

She died the day he died. We buried her on the same day we buried Rob, as he lay on sheepskin in his rimu coffin. We scattered rosemary on his casket and she was in there with him, curled up in the crook of his arm, holding his hand.

The woman who stood by his grave looking down as he was lowered into the earth was a different person. She was exposed to the elements, her skin and her mind flayed open, her eyes the colour of the storm, her heart filled with sadness.

But, over time, she learned to build a new mind, a new skin. Her heart would never change its shape, but it stopped tearing apart with grief. There is a price for surviving that, and part of the price is not knowing what parts of me survived, and what parts are completely new.

I am myself, but I don't fully understand myself yet. What are my limits? What broke irreparably? What is stronger?

When I think about Dog Paw, I wonder if I'm picking people I can't get close to on purpose.

Maybe it's that, the more time goes on, I am coming to the sinking realisation that I may never enter into a long-term relationship again.

~

The last time I saw Dog Paw, which was a week before I left for my big trip, I thought about this need we have to attribute value to something.

I recall Puja's words, how everything has to serve a purpose that shows you are economically successful.

If it's a job, it's about the company you work for, the job title you hold. If it's a relationship, it's about the ring on your finger, the house you buy. If it's your child, it's what school she goes to, what grades he gets.

Dog Paw is an emerging musician, and like most people who are starting out, he juggles jobs to fund the thing he is passionate about. He is clever and funny, but because of his age, he hasn't yet acquired that filter where your brain edits what's going to be interesting as a story. Listening to him is sometimes exhausting.

Factoring in Dog Paw's age, the fact that I am going away

for eight months, and the creeping suspicion that he's just fulfilling a boyhood crush he once had on Amara Karan, the Indian actress in *The Darjeeling Limited*, this is probably the last time I'm going to see him.

But as we spend our last evening together, I learn that intimacy is not the exclusive preserve of a relationship. Because whatever this is, for a moment, after the fire is lit and the blaze roars through our bodies, in the embers, there is connection.

He plays the guitar afterwards. He's resurrecting chords from a memory, but because he has not yet pulled them into a song, they are fragmented clouds, scattered. He hasn't yet gathered them into a thing that will tell the skies what shape it will be.

Outside this room, people will try to tell us what this is. They will look at his age, and at mine, and they will form stories of what they think this should be – what it cannot be.

He is a beautiful musician; his melody renders me quiet.

Perhaps this is where I learn about the realms of words and silence, and realise the true power the latter has. Not articulating what I am feeling, but letting the emotion wash over me is sometimes more powerful than words.

At that point, hair mussed, the imprint of him on my skin, I am held still and quiet in the moment of it, my body stretched across the bed, just the sound of strings and its beauty washing over me.

I look at him, his fingers moving across the fretboard, lost in his own reverie.

I wonder about emptiness and loneliness. I wonder how much he will feel after we have parted ways, what are the ballasts in his life and what would push him to love someone so much, in the way that I loved Rob? I think every human being is capable of it, the immensity of that kind of love, the warmth of it, the comfort.

I think about myself, finding affection in temporary places. I think about the currency of love, the hierarchies and status we attribute to it. Where a night with a man much younger than me, conducted in absolute honesty, with tenderness and laughter, is viewed as less valuable than entire lifetimes conducted by people whose relationships tug at the strings of dishonesty.

The chords start to quieten; the piece of music is coming to an end.

Although I am half pulling away, wondering how to disappear like motes of dust through the window because I know that I cannot feel anything resembling permanence towards him, I will remember the sweetness of this moment and how it made me feel for some time to come.

~

'We're here, ma'am,' says Susheel, smiling with teeth stained red with the betel nut he's been chewing the whole way.

After driving down a narrow and treacherous path, we arrive at Tyrna, the village where you can hire a guide to take you to the double-decker root bridge.

Susheel asks me if I want him to recommend me a guide,

and here is where I learn about not being a presump-
tuous dick.

The standard operating procedure in India is that, as a
visitor, you expect everyone to be running some sort of con,
like a nationwide version of *Ocean's Eleven* where the goal
is to dupe the dumb tourist.

You have money and most people don't. There are a lot
of people who do the morality maths of swindling you
out of your fat-cat Western currency to feed their starving
family, and it's a no-brainer.

If you are a regular traveller to India, you expect to be
shafted almost by default.

But what I've noticed is that there is a higher incidence of
this happening in urban areas, where there are more people
and the stakes of desperation are higher.

Obviously, however, this is only a percentage of the pop-
ulation. In the more rural areas especially, they are kind,
helpful and are trying to eke out a living as the rest of us are.

On this day, I forget this. I instantly assume that Susheel
recommending a guide means he's working some scam. I
find out quite quickly that he isn't.

Most people, especially Indian tourists, don't want to
pay out for a guide, so they attempt it alone, and some
twits – one in particular we passed along the way – reach
the first bridge – a metal suspension bridge – and think
that's it. Or they reach the second one that is also a suspension bridge but has the beginnings of a fledgling root
bridge around it, and turn back. Also people are just

fucking lazy and want to walk the least distance for their Instagram shot.

At the drop-off point, there are guides clamouring around, little kids selling bamboo poles and a tiny café selling food at the entrance. He finds a guide – a small young man by the name of Steady.

Steady is dressed in neat Nike tracksuit bottoms and a long-sleeved top. He tells me the rate for his services to take me to the village of Nongriat where the bridge is located, and I bark at him, 'That seems like a lot', to squash any chance of being cheated. He looks confused and I see there is a fixed-rate sign, and he's telling me the truth. I am such a dick.

The entrance to the village is humble: tiny houses and gardens, steps that begin as we pass people's front yards. Most people know Steady, and they say hello.

We bound down the steps, passing little houses along the way. I'm amazed at how clean everything is.

We pass women studiously weeding their steps. One guy is brushing his teeth on the porch of his house. There is a lot of activity going on in the way of washing pots outdoors in wide, cement sinks, clothes are being thwacked against stone and front yards are being swept.

We start our descent down a long flight of stairs. Butterflies greet us: bright-blue and white spots, mustard yellow. One flaps past lazily on wings the colour of storm water.

All around us are mountains, dipping and soaring into a sweep of green: fat fronds and trees necklaced in spider webs.

Two women dressed in Khasi style – elegant sheets of sari fabric draped over them – pass us by; they are followed by a trail of scent: woodsmoke, tea and soap. Their faces are unreadable – I wonder what they think of all these tourists tramping through.

Only 30–40 per cent of people who come here make it to the bridge – most are too out of shape to do the whole thing and some, grown soft from always being ferried around in a car or taking the escalator, require a palanquin because they grossly underestimate how much effort it takes to climb back up the stairs.

Steady tells me that the villagers like the publicity because it creates business, but at the same time, having that many people coming through is also a pain.

This path is used to connect Nongriat to the outside world – it can't be accessed by car. We pass people going about their everyday jobs, carrying cement, wood – everything and anything they need to survive.

'They work very hard,' says Steady. Although there are mobile networks and Wi-Fi, when the villagers need to bring their produce to take to market, they have to shut the trail and use a special pulley system to transport the goods.

We reach our first suspension bridge, crossing pools languid and blue in places, broken up with the rush of water teeming onwards. Soon enough, we arrive at a homestead that announces the root bridge is imminent. We stop for a rest on the side of the wall.

Steady tells me he is studying at university; I know he

doesn't have much money, and it must take a lot for him to be able to do that. Like the rest of his people, he works very hard.

There are a few people milling around. A little girl is placed in a hammock, her mother desperately hoping she will stay in it this time. But two minutes later, the child emancipates herself and makes a beeline for the dog half-heartedly guarding the front of a small house.

Steady knows these people too. An elderly lady with a face like an apple collapsing in on itself takes his face in both hands and tells me he's a 'good boy'. Soon, we head on.

The root bridge comes upon us quietly. I almost don't notice it at first because we enter a clearing with a clear pool of water at its centre. The start of the bridge looks like a tree having a yawn; it spreads angular at first, then wild and covered in moss, over and over the water until it touches the other side.

The first reaction is shock, that I'm here looking at the incredible thing I came all this way for. Feeling wonder, relief, happiness, I run my hand along the root. It took years to build this, I think. I feel the slow pulse of the trees, their life source, their lungs.

I understand why people think the only thing that can fix a heart broken by love is another love equal or greater in magnitude.

But that doesn't have to come from just one other person. When you think about all of the love you will ever experience in your lifetime, including that which you have for yourself, that is still an immense foundation to build your life on.

This feeling, under the bright Indian sky, with this sprawl of nature around me, and gladness in my heart that I did something as simple as walk down 3,000 steps to see a bridge made out of roots, this feeling trickles between the cracks to mend the damage.

Maybe I will never again be brave enough to love someone as much as I did Rob. Maybe I will never allow my heart to be broken again.

But I know that if I do, and if it does happen, finding the way to heal within myself and the nature that surrounds me is going to sustain me a lot longer than finding that answer in another person.

7

WOODSMOKE, FIRE AND ICE

A few months ago, I was shocked to read that only around 5 per cent of our brain activity is conscious. The rest of our decision-making, how we react to things, process grief, happiness, worry, mostly takes place backstage.

Back when the figure was estimated at around 10 per cent, newspapers jumped on it and incorrectly said, 'We only use 10 per cent of our brain!' What it really meant was that, when it comes to the majority of your thinking about who you are as a person, you are a covert military facility with hundreds of sub-levels.

The vast, subterranean version of myself fascinates me. I imagine her swimming deep beneath my eyes, occasionally reminded of her existence with the gleam of a fin discernible above water before she slips down below.

I was most conscious of her when Rob died, because she was the one who kicked my survival into gear on so many unknown levels. I've felt her before, of course, and it's always marked by the same process:

- A very firm sense of what I need to do.
- My conscious brain kicking against the decision.
- Not understanding it but feeling compelled to go through with it.
- Understanding it once it has been undertaken and completed.

I have a heavy cold, and I have temporarily left behind India for Nepal, for a much-needed dose of solitude. But subterranean me is trying to get me to leave our comfortable hotel room, and this time I feel she has gone too far.

To go a bit further back as to why I came here, as much as I love India, and have come to know her quieter side, her frantic buzz is like a needy friend. After a while, she is cloying; she robs the oxygen from beneath my nose and I feel like I am trapped and can't breathe.

I knew I wanted and needed Nepal long before I came here. I wanted to be in the mountains for two weeks, and scrolling on a website I came across a trek that promised exactly that, 'from steaming jungle to icy snow caps', and I could do it alone. I didn't know then that it was the Annapurna base camp trek, or the ABC circuit – one of the most famous in the world.

When I found out, at first I thought, 'Argh! I don't want to go on some trek crawling with people! The whole point was to get away from the fuckers!' But the more I read, the more I understood that young backpackers tended not to do it because of the cost. Those seeking glory did Everest base camp, and so, while busy, it tended to be a mixed bag of people who mostly couldn't speak English.

Since I couldn't speak any other language, this was pretty much perfect.

We have a couple of days in Kathmandu to acclimatise before the trek, and, so far, I had turned down all offers of sightseeing. But when the guiding company I booked asked me again if I was SURE I didn't want to visit their biggest temple, this subconscious part of me manipulated my lips to say yes and swallowed a couple of Sudafed.

Her insistence reminds me of a quote by Rabindranath Tagore, India's first Nobel laureate, which goes, 'What seems to be coming at you is really coming from you.'

The thing is, I don't like visiting temples. Why? Because I'm angry at God. I know the logic follows that I'm an atheist and therefore I don't believe in God, so I might as well be angry at a sock puppet, but I'm still angry.

I'm angry at whatever idea of God I had before I became an atheist. I'm angry that I don't believe. I'm angry that prayer and belief and God in general did nothing to save Rob's life.

Maybe God isn't in the life-saving business, but I'm not interested in second-guessing on God's behalf. I have never understood the logic of the believer trying to interpret the actions of an omnipotent being, whose existence surely is beyond the understanding of a tiny human peanut brain.

But that could be the anger in me. After a suicide, there are casualties in the form of lost friendships and family rifts.

I am still angry with some people, but that pales in comparison to my anger with God. God and me are not okay.

It takes a lot for me to enter God's home – whether it be a temple, church, synagogue or mosque.

~

Kathmandu is crowded, but it is a different kind of noise and activity to Kolkata, where I have just been.

Kolkata, in my opinion, is a place over-romanticised in guidebooks. It used to be the capital of India during the time of the Raj, and nowhere in India is there a city of such decay yet immense learning, life and graft. People talk about decay as if it is a jaunty quirk to be admired – in the same way they talk about Palermo in Sicily – but all I see is the presence of time in its saddest form: blackened buildings, weeds snaking through pieces of stone, creaking, cracking, everything releasing a dusty sigh for days gone past.

We saw the buildings created in our imaginations as we read them from pages of books: crumbling intricate frontages, porticos reclaimed by leaves and roots, green wooden shutters inspired by the French set in deep red-clay walls. Every inch of pavement in some places is occupied: men fixing watches, sharpening knives, recycling bits of scrap metal. Every so often we'd come across a vat of bubbling oil and stare as flattened discs of dough placed expertly in their liquid emerged reborn as the softest, flakiest breads.

I went with Rob's aunt Felicity who had joined me from New Zealand for two weeks, and the heat flickered uncomfortably under our skins. It was hard to reconcile this great centre of culture and creative thinking, the birthplace of Tagore and Satyajit Ray, with the random guy who blew his nose onto a wall, the constant press of people, the staring that Felicity elicited, and the women who were poured into traditional shalwar kameezes, not skinny jeans like they are in Bangalore.

To go from that, straight into the different yet still chaotic streets of Kathmandu, where dust and traffic compete with hundreds of shops selling trekking gear, statues of Buddha and parcels of weed, my brain overloads. The city is five thousand years old and so the lanes are narrow and unprepared, groaning with cars and progress.

To try to escape the noise, I'm receptive to getting out of the city centre. Until I hear it's a visit to the Pashupatinath temple. I Google it and my mind recoils: they do open-air cremations.

In Hinduism, traditionally you are cremated within a wooden pyre, but these days most people use the standard crematoriums. When I was a believer, I was a strong advocate of open-air cremations – it's what I wanted for my own death.

Wooden pyre, open sky and the river at my feet.

But it seemed grisly, gruesome, that this was a place open to tourists. It seemed like the ultimate 'fuck you' to grieving people so that privileged Western masses could come to take pictures.

I also didn't know how I would handle seeing a dead body, as the last body I had seen was Rob's.

So when my guide Sushma comes to pick me up, I am wriggling with indecision.

But this other me insists I should go, and I instantly like Sushma because there is something familiar about her features, her mannerisms. She reminds me of my aunts.

On the drive there, Sushma and I chat, and the question inevitably comes: are you married? So I take a deep breath and tell her about Rob. And as is the way sometimes when I talk about Rob, our conversation grows more thoughtful, and I feel Sushma bending towards me, not away. I usually find this in people who have encountered death before.

When we arrive at the entrance, there aren't hordes of tourists. Pashupati, as it is shortened to, is first and foremost a working temple, not a tourist site. So the majority of people visiting are here for legitimate reasons of devotion, not just to take photographs. Foreigners aren't allowed inside the temple either, and they have to pay 1,000NPR just to visit the outer grounds, which is a lot just to see a temple.

Sushma wangles free entry for me because Indians have a good relationship in Nepal, and basically get all of the same rights as Nepalese tourists. So maybe the last 'fuck you' was being had at the West's expense.

The heavy, stone cremation slabs sit alongside the river on the opposite side to us, the final resting place to countless bodies. No judgement, just peace and quiet. There is a fire dying out on one, and further along we see a body garlanded in marigolds, the loved ones gathering around for a last goodbye.

In the background is the temple, and, all along our side of the bank, it is peaceful.

Sadhus daubed in sandalwood and vermillion lounge coquettishly asking if we want to take their picture. Other people sit under the trees near us, gazing at the process of life and death unfolding.

Along the bank, we can see the heat of the fires rippling the air, and as we see yet another body tightly wrapped in flowers and cloth making its way to another stone slab, we sit quietly and take in the moment.

Sushma presses my shoulder in comfort, reflective with what I have already told her about Rob. We look at the one slab where the fire has now completely died out, and a young man collects water from the river. 'We cremated my father right there,' she says.

We grow quiet again, and I am not crying; I am surprised. Far from this being an upsetting place, it is incredibly healing. There is something about death being out in the open, in the same place that people are praying for love, for hope, for babies and for health, that articulates the hugeness and fullness of life in a way that words cannot.

'We believe in death as being a return to the five elements,' Sushma says. I cannot tell her about how angry I am with God, because she is religious. And that it has been creeping on me that maybe I am not an atheist after all, because how can you be angry at something that isn't there?

'It is the earth, sky, water, air and fire,' she says. And in that moment, the young man takes his bucket of water and throws it on the ashes. The water douses fire, blowing steam into the air which evaporates into the sky. The ashes plume up and then fall into the water, and into the cracks of the earth. That person is still here, I think, but now they are part of something more ambiguous, less defined, but still part of the moving and breathing world.

I wonder how small or big that person was. I wonder if they led a good life, if they realised that life was precious, that inevitably we all end up with our eyes closed, our time ended and our bodies emptied of purpose.

Sushma tells me that further down the bank is the cheap and cheerful crematorium that is more environmentally friendly and only costs 300NPR. The traditional cremations are far more expensive because they require 300kg of wood, and take hours to complete.

I was worried the air would smell of burning flesh, but actually, it is filled with incense and wood. She tells me that when a husband dies, the widow has to do various things like not eat meat or food with salt and sleep on a plank of wood – as must the sons.

'And when the wife dies?' I say, raising an eyebrow, because I think I know what's coming. 'Ah,' says Sushma, 'he doesn't have to do any of that stuff.'

Of course he bloody doesn't. Widowhood always hits a nerve because, in India, you're supposed to wear white. No chicken nuggets for you – it's vegetarian food all the way – and back when you lived in big houses stuffed with your extended family, you slept in your own cursed wing. Away from the kids, marrieds and single folk.

If you were really unlucky, you might be cast out. Some widows were forced to go into prostitution because they had no other means of making money. Can you imagine having to go through the intense pain of losing your husband, then go through the second, devastating blow of being ostracised and shunned?

When Felicity and I did our walking tour of Kolkata, we came across a beautiful old mansion. Our guide Ritik showed us different wings in the courtyard and pointed at one wing saying, 'That's where the widows would live and eat, and they would have to use different utensils so their food wouldn't get contaminated by the non-vegetarian pots.'

Delightful.

A sadhu peeps his head around a corner, waggling his eyebrows smeared in bright yellow, touting for money. 'Picture?' he asks.

We take that as our cue to leave, and we head towards the temple. Only Hindus are allowed, and we leave the foreigners, with their SLRs and iPhones, behind, to enter into a world of marigolds and betel leaves, incense smoke and old statues that depict the playing ground of the gods.

The temple is the opposite of the riverbank. It teems with life and colour. It tugs at a string of memory.

When I was a kid, I used to love temples, and especially loved the elephant god Ganesh. I was given a tiny stone statue of him, and I had it for so long his face rubbed off.

Ganesh stands for a lot of things, but he is also called the 'remover of obstacles' and Rob loved statues and depictions of him.

When Rob went to New Zealand just after we separated, I gave it to him. I don't know why. I think – despite being an atheist – I wanted something to look over him, protect him. When he died, I found the statue among his belongings and tucked it next to him in the coffin.

'Make sure that wherever he wanted to get to, that he gets there safely,' I murmured to Ganesh.

In Pashupati, you can feel the sense of hope in the air. Pashupati is actually an incarnation of the blue-skinned god Shiva, who is one of the trinity of the most powerful Hindu gods, the others being Brahma the creator and Vishnu the preserver.

He's also Ganesh's father. Shiva is especially liked by women because a) he's got this godly yet edgy and dangerous vibe and b) he has the most gorgeous, sensual, intelligent relationship with his wife Parvati.

Reason (c) is a bit more complicated and best explained in the words of our Kolkata walking tour guide, Ritik. He coughed and went red when Felicity and I stopped in front of the most beautiful Shiva lingam peeping out between the folds of a banyan tree.

The lingam is a version of a Shiva statue that is a black column rounded at the end. When you're a kid, you just think it's a funny-looking stone. It was only when we were older that we were told what it symbolised.

'*Ahem*, so the lingam ... *ahem* ... represents the god Shiva, *ahem* ...' Ritik said.

I started sniggering because I knew what was coming; Felicity patiently listened, unaware.

'And the lingam itself ... *ahem ahem* ... represents his ... *ahem* ... penis.'

Felicity's eyebrows shot up. What Ritik didn't say was that the base, or *onni*, actually represents a woman's vagina, and it's usually a circle in the ground around the lingam.

Encouraged by the fact that we hadn't started laughing outright yet, Ritik continued: 'Women pray to the lingam when they want to have a child or if ... they want their future husband to have a ... *ahem* ...'

I put him out of his misery: 'A big penis?' Felicity's cackle met with mine sent the crows cawing above the trees.

In Nepal, they are big on Shiva. The lingam in Pashupati is so huge, you have to descend a few stairs to see it. It is penis central. As we ascend, we pass a worn and loved statue of Hanuman, the monkey god, and then reach the central temple that holds other statues of Shiva.

Sushma takes my hand and leads me to the temple of another god, called Unmatta Bhairava. 'This one used to scare me as a child,' she says.

I enter the small, dark room and see a fearsome face, the style of work resembling more the statues I've seen in Malaysia and Bali than India. This god, I later find out, is the one people pray to for strength to be brave and bold.

Apparently, he's also like visual Viagra − if you're

impotent or not sexually attracted to your partner any more, one look at him and *bing!* You get your mojo back.

Sushma points at a particular part of the statue and, in the gloom, I can see people circle the statue and give this long brass object a good old rub like it grants instant wishes. As we get closer, I see Sushma's delicate hand reach out for it and realise, *Oh, yep, that's a massive metal wang and this lady who looks like a sweet old Indian auntie is grabbing it for good luck.*

When we walk out of the temple, something in my centre of gravity has shifted.

This anger, this blame – I'm not saying that I still don't have it.

I'm angry Rob was taken away from me. I'm angry that he died before his time and was given such a tough road to walk down. But after experiencing the confluence of those deaths on the riverbank and the striving for a better life, I also now have the realisation that there isn't anything personal in Rob dying.

There is a soft voice, mine, that comes from a place of understanding.

It wasn't about him, this is just how it is, how it always will be as long as we honour the living and the dead.

It doesn't make things easier – not hugely anyway. I still feel the sadness of his death around me, but I also feel like we are part of something bigger.

I still don't believe in God, but something in this experience has allowed me to break the earth around my anger, to start letting it go because it's preventing me from moving on.

Finally the understanding dawns that we are connected so deeply to this world we live on – all of it – and that somewhere, somehow, there is a sense of peace and closure, and healing, in this.

~

I left England feeling indignant that non-traditional life choices weren't celebrated, and that even if you follow a more traditional path, you aren't equipped with the insight to question, think and learn about why you make the choices you do.

At the beginning, I was so sure that, to live the life I wanted, I'd have to remove myself from people. That to be free of judgement and to live in peace, I would have to surround myself with silence.

However, that led me down another warren of thinking. Was I rejecting the idea of marriage and kids because I believed it was expected of me? And, in doing so, was I allowing other people's expectations to shape me anyway? What if I ended up bitter and lonely and realised too late that it was all a mistake? And why couldn't people just respect the choices you made, whether that was to actively live alone or to remain single?

Someone who has written a lot about this is Eric Klinenberg, the professor of sociology and director of the Institute for Public Knowledge at New York University. He wrote a book called *Going Solo*, which looks at the rise and appeal of living alone. I liked what the *Washington Post* said about it, that it was 'really about living better together – for all of us, single or not'.

To me, there was a distinction between making an active choice to live alone versus a default choice because I hadn't met someone. One was empowering; the other was just waiting on the shelf like a toy waiting to be picked up.

I emailed Eric to ask him why some people had such a problem with other people living alone, and he revealed that human beings have only been living alone in large numbers, for long periods of time, in the past sixty years, which is a blink in the eye of our evolution.

He told me that we have a whole bunch of expectations for what a good life is like, and how it should be lived, developed solely in that world. And that the experience of being alone is radical and transformative, and it's new in ways we haven't thought of.

'It's new for people to understand, especially your family,' he wrote back. 'They have a clear idea of what a good life is, and you're not living it. It doesn't come from bad intentions, it's really just that our cultural practices have not caught up with the way that we live now.'

Eric told me about what sociologists refer to as the 'spoiled identity', which is that there is one lens that people see you through, and they can't see outside of that. I wonder if married people feel like that about themselves, not just single folk.

But, I replied to Eric, sometimes I felt like I would talk to certain people about my life or my choices, and was met with a certain level of incomprehension.

Well, yes, he said, because people don't often listen.

'They don't take the time to appreciate the reasons you are living by yourself or not married or are single. So often they are projecting their own feelings, that is: "If I was not married, I would be really unhappy", and there can be real misunderstanding. A lot of single people have come to resent those interactions.'

While it might take a bit longer for society to catch up with different ways of living, dealing with the irritation of it might be simpler than we think.

He advises that recognising that people are projecting their concerns onto you, and understanding that they are generally asking because they care, matters.

I spent months beating myself up because I truly believed that I wasn't going to be happy again, because my life didn't match the lives of other people. But perhaps I wasn't thinking big enough. Or, perhaps, we all needed to update what we thought we knew about modern living.

Eric told me something that still plays on my mind today, which is that our ideas and values aren't in sync with how we live our lives. That we're pretty much going to spend about as much of our lives single as we are married, which is a new thing.

The simple act of acknowledging that there is no perfect system, and that, actually, there is no 'them and us' – we're all in the same, messy jumble – can offer incredible clarity to your own life. To me, it's oxygen. It allows for flaws, mistakes, room to fuck up and start over again.

It lances the boil filled with jealous comparisons.

I sat there on that riverbank watching a life go up in flames, and, in that fire, I saw a reconciling of my own anger. There is no set path to happiness, and even those who follow the rules may end up somewhere they hadn't planned, because shit happens and things go wrong.

There was only so much I could blame for me not having kids, for instance, on Rob. Or being jealous of people who did have kids or a seemingly normal marriage. I had to take charge of my own narrative.

~

The last message I send Mum and Dad which will have to tide them over for the next two weeks is: 'Heading out to the mountains, no reception, DON'T WORRY!! Feeling good and strong.'

They do not need to know that I am still heavy with a cold, barely able to taste anything and that my river of snot could replenish an ailing glacier.

The set-up is this: I have my guide Suman, a young Nepalese man-child, who takes great pride in his hair. Suman has a strange combination of being young yet world-weary – he's been doing this for a few years and thinks he knows everything, but is actually just a boy.

When we set out, I stop to peer at a bird in the tree, but

can't quite make out what species it is. Rob would have known, but he is no longer human enough to answer me; he is simply scattered cloud and wisps of air.

'What is that?' I ask Suman, pointing. I naively assume, being a trekking guide, that Suman will have a great knowledge of everything nature.

He looks, nods, and says sagely, 'Yes, bird.'

Rob, I miss you.

The guides need to be fairly physically fit. They accompany people like me for two weeks at a time with not much rest, and the trek is physically demanding. There are long days, and it is up and down. The altitude takes its toll – sometimes you can clear 1,000 metres vertically, and the oxygen level is poor.

The guide isn't there to unlock the frost-tipped mysteries of the Nepalese Himalayas; he's there to negotiate a bed for you in one of the rustic teahouses that mark the way up. The higher you go, the fewer teahouses there are and so the demand for beds is a scuffle.

It becomes evident that you need a guide who can help get your food quickly, your bed sorted, and make sure you don't die from altitude sickness. Bird and plant life knowledge are a surplus requirement.

We start in Pokhara, a pretty mountain town set around a lake.

Stretching ahead down the path, like wooden fingers straining to deliver a letter, the trees are caught against the cool embrace of a bright blue sky. Up ahead, casting a watchful eye on the dense undergrowth, is an eagle – or bird, as Suman would say – with white spots on its wings.

After a short drive, we start the trail.

~

There is a lot of literature around about self-love. One lady wrote an article saying that she tried practising it, but felt 'guilty' that she spent her whole weekend eating pastries and watching Netflix, while her other half ran around after her. That's not what self-love is.

Self-love is one of the hardest things you can do. We have this idea of love being easy and effortless, and sometimes it is. But love isn't one-dimensional; it doesn't just operate on one plane of emotion. Love is a state of being, and operates to the full gamut of feeling, from anger to bliss, happiness to angst.

There are parts of yourself that will always be easier to love than others. Maybe it's your kindness, your way of making people laugh. But real self-love (which, really, is self-acceptance) is also being fully conscious and aware of the darker parts of you. It's looking at the parts of yourself you really don't like. The parts that may cause you to self-destruct when shit gets tough and lead you to make bad decisions.

Often, these things aren't obvious, which is why you keep doing it despite evidence to the contrary that it's good for you. The behaviour is not black and white or good and bad, like, say, someone who throws cats into a dustbin or volunteers in soup kitchens. It's the insidious stuff that presses down on your life, that causes you to act out in certain ways.

It might be an inability to say no to people. Always doing good deeds because you want people to think well of you, despite the steep emotional cost to yourself. It could be wanting love but finding it in the wrong places. Your darker self is a master at covering its tracks so you never realise it is even there.

Self-love is saying to yourself, 'This thing that I am doing is ugly and it hurts, but it's *me* and I need to find out what it is so I can stop making the same mistakes.'

The reason I love trekking, or rather, being around mountains, is that there is no hiding from my bullshit. I can't get on my phone to distract me from an uncomfortable thought. There is a lot of thinking to do, and it happens at its own pace and timeline.

Some self-love revelations are forced because of a trauma. Mine certainly were after Rob died. But mountains offer a gentler path to understanding yourself, without the need for a catastrophe.

Because the life around them is slower, less accessible (and therefore much more magnificent, beautiful and rare), you feel as if you are in the presence of something divine. Not God, but something taps into the truest parts of yourself and amplifies who you are as a person, threading it into gold.

Most of us, in towns and cities, are used to close quarters. We are used to speed, accessibility – I freak out when I have no service on my phone for five minutes.

So being here, in this landscape, forces a change. In the spaces of silence we finally hear a voice that is our own. It comes unbidden, softly, willingly, not through trauma or coaxed through the words of a therapist or a friend delivering tough love.

It's difficult, unsettling at first. An hour in, and I realise there are many, many hours, minutes and seconds between this first hour and the last one.

Unless you are with a guide who can speak perfect English and is chatty, there is a lot of walking and thinking. During a lot of the 'thinking' part of this trek, I think about the person I was in London.

Was I a nice person? Did I treat people right? People said I did when I left my company, but I remember meetings when the fire of a red rage blew through me and I ended up losing my temper.

Did I leave because I didn't like the person I was becoming? Thinking about it in the silence of the jungle, with my thoughts radiating out towards the mountains, there is no one to give me the answer but myself.

I don't think I was terrible, but perhaps I could have been better.

~

'4.30am!!' I yell at Suman. When was he going to tell me we had such an early start?

It wasn't the point that I'd be in bed by 8pm anyway, and my night-time activity involved gumming a piece of Lindt chocolate while wearing my cosy Tibetan socks. I wanted more notice. Then I guiltily remember my promise to be nicer and more Zen and back off.

The reason for the early start is to climb up to Poon Hill, a detour up a mini mountain to see the sunrise. *This is the revelatory shit you signed up for, Poorna, so suck it up.*

When the alarm goes off, I don't want to leave, even less so five minutes into the dark hike, up a set of stairs so steep they swell to fill your entire sense of physical being until all you breathe, think and see are stairs. I have a tantrum around twenty stairs in and decide, nope, I am not going to do it.

But then, I take my eyes off the ground where they have studiously been following the drag of my torchlight, and I look up. The world shifts into that other place, where co-ordinates melt and it is so otherworldly and beautiful you are scared to take your eyes off it, in case it disappears while you blink.

Because we are on a path via a small Nepalese village, and because there are no cars, no skyscrapers, everything on either side of the path cuts away and moves towards the mountains.

We find ourselves surrounded on all sides by stars, millions of them, some peppering the blackness with fire and pomp, others shyly grouping together as if not convinced they could shine brightly enough on their own. I look out at our galaxy and I feel as if I could lose myself forever in its glow.

I've never hiked in the dark before; everything takes on

a different tone. The staircase is framed in curly branches of small rhododendrons, their limbs jerking into shadowy movement as the light hits.

The night landscape is so different to its daytime counterpart that hiking in the dark feels as if we are having a secret affair, poring over each other before the day comes to claim me. Eventually, I get to the top and catch the sun calling to the stars.

The sky dips its brush and begins in a slow dark blue, lightening into spears of red, drawing a line under the night. In the background, a legion of mountains wait silently. As the first rays of the sun hit them one by one, they move from the shadows into vision, their lines rippling across a previously unformed place, now shaped by warmth and light into peaks of stone and ice.

The smallness of me, and the vastness of this, quietens my very core.

Later that day, as we move onwards and upwards to Tadapani, I notice how different a trek this is to the last one I did nearly two years ago in New Zealand.

There, I found myself wanting to melt into mist, through the veil of lace created by branches in the distance. I wanted it to claim me, for me to turn to stone and have moss growing on my legs and ferns from my fingers.

This is more conscious, more present. I'm not a spirit passing through the world with a detached gaze; I'm here, my thighs are on fucking fire and every step is working the sweat and sadness of London out of me.

We enter dense woodland and jungle, the air growing so hot that clouds evaporate into steam.

I pass across steps cut through with running water, each stream merely the idea of a waterfall, the gathering trickle sharing a collective dream of one day thundering along the mountainside.

I think of Rob, I think of *taniwha*, the beings and guardians from Maori mythology who liked to live in watery places, from the sea to rock pools. Sometimes they could be created from the spirit of someone who had died; he loved their stories.

We pass many streams along the way, and I place a stone near each one to say hello to him, just in case. *Tell him I was here,* I whisper into the water.

High up in the canopy of trees, bees are making a life; rhododendrons give them the pollen that creates a very special honey.

The waterfalls give way to thickets of trees. We pass avenues of rhododendrons, their desperation evident in the way they are clawing at the light. Here the light has shepherded sturdy beech across a wide valley so that they are all clamouring towards it. It is a sea of wood, rippling downwards.

The trunks of trees flutter with the skeletons of dead ferns. The branches are a needlework of moss.

Eventually, we hit a ridge where the clouds roll directly onto our path; they taste like the edge of something delicate and wet.

We stop for black tea to remove the taste of clouds from

our tongues, and, as we get up to leave, there is a sight that stops my heart.

Having Rob in my thoughts for most of the day (it is that kind of day), there is a shaft of light that turns the furthest crease of the mountains into a shimmer, a promise of a different place where he might be.

I don't think I will ever stop feeling like this, as if he is so nearby I could almost reach out my hand and feel him reach out for me on the other side.

Despite my independence, despite this being a journey about me and not my grief, there is something about the gathering of mountains and silence that makes every part of my soul cry this question to the skies: Will I ever love and be loved again?

~

Google isn't just a search engine; it reveals some of the most hidden, vulnerable and human parts of ourselves. I'm talking about auto-complete, the function that tries to finish off a question you're typing by suggesting the most commonly searched phrases.

'Will I fall ...' immediately prompts: 'Will I fall in love again'. 'Why does love ...' immediately prompts: 'Why does love hurt'. So here we are, yearning for an answer about something so personal to ourselves, from an algorithm. We want there to be rules so that we can follow them and, that way, mitigate being hurt.

We try to instil order in a primary emotion that has no

intention of playing by the rules. We say it should give us certain things, it should fix illnesses, it should make us happy, but the truth is: it never promised to do that.

Although I had a big love with Rob, I felt utterly lost when it came to thinking about my future and the part love played in it once he was gone. I knew my expectation of love, before I met Rob, was that it would fix everything, and it would last for ever. It's a hugely popular line of thinking, but one that doesn't bear up when that love fails or dies.

Before I left on my big trip, I emailed Daniel Jones, who has edited the *New York Times*' 'Modern Love' column for thirteen years – a beloved fixture for showcasing all the intricacies, complications, betrayals and reunions of love. I wanted to know whether he had noticed patterns in the way people approached thinking about love.

He wrote back that we tended to try to follow scripts in life. 'Those scripts – wedding, marriage, children – don't allow for a lot of variety. I have seen couples break up over infidelity – even when they don't want to – because that's what people do, essentially, and that's what others expect. It's hard to cut your own path.

'But one of the biggest problems in terms of how we view love is the way we often think of it as a feeling. As something we can't control. And as long as we feel good about someone, we're in love. But love is really about active caring, active curiosity – choice. Love isn't passive, and people who treat it that way aren't likely to hold onto that feeling for very long.'

I wanted to know about marriage. Mainly because I want to know if I got it wrong. 'We used to marry for other reasons – practical, religious, political,' he says. 'Now we marry for love, and supposedly we stay together for love, but that's a lot of pressure.

'We don't need each other in the ways we used to, so love is our sole bond. A better question for newly married people might be: What are our expectations for how we are going to try to be kind and helpful to each other going forward?'

I think about Daniel's words over and over with each hour, each clomp on a tree root, every step up and down. I turn them over carefully like pearls.

When I think about why people get married, why I got married, it's because I saw it as the ultimate declaration of my love for Rob. I loved him, and so obviously marriage was our natural end point, right? Except, a marriage requires a lot more than just love.

Commitment was never our problem or the doubt that we could and wanted to be together for the years we never ended up having; it was all the other messy stuff that tied into his illnesses. A big part undoubtedly was that Rob felt he couldn't tell me that he wasn't the man I thought I'd married because maybe I wouldn't want to be with the real him. I don't know that he understood that the lies were far more damaging than the actual reality of himself.

I'm fairly sure that I won't remarry, and, admittedly, a small part of that is because the prospect of meeting someone to seriously date them seems so impossible. But the biggest part is because, while I loved being called his wife, and there is something about marriage that deepens a bond, I don't know that I want to build a life with someone in that way.

I'm capable of love – I know that in my bones. But I don't know if I'm capable of setting aside my life, to become part of theirs in that all-consuming way. And I don't feel like I need to do it to be socially acceptable to others.

Once I remove the idea of having it again, it releases the pressure like a whistle.

~

We continue. There are leaves, brushed along the branches of trees as if by a miniaturist, gentle and fine.

Around the trunks are fronds of some beautiful parasite, its leaves descending haughtily like a beggared aristocrat down the length like a spiral staircase. Millet and grasses cover the downward slopes in a melt of yellow and green, bursting into gold when the sun is allowed glory from behind the clouds. Along the darker paths, more beech trees, this time growing in a less ordered tangle.

At various teahouses, I meet a lot of different people. Trekkers in the region can be on different circuits – not everyone is headed to base camp – and some people go at a different pace to others. There are also several teahouses clustered in the same area, and there's not a guarantee you will always see the same people in the same teahouse. The guides also seem to work to their own structure of loyalty, so there are some restaurants and teahouses they will visit, others they won't.

This set-up places a lot of emphasis on human connection. You know the ones you get on with, and the ones you don't. A chance encounter with someone you like might brighten the rest of your day. There is no TV and no phone, so something as simple as watching kids on a homemade Ferris wheel is hugely thrilling. And concerning: the Ferris wheel is made from blocks of wood that look like they are going to spin off into the mountains at any moment.

We watch a dog chasing a cat chasing a rabbit and, at that moment, it's better than an Oscar-nominated film.

I name my walking sticks Thelma and Louise. At one point, Louise loses the protective cap on her pointy end and she ends up picking up leaves like I'm doing community service in a park. Sometimes they get stuck in rocks, but they save my knees, which collapse around day eight.

Around 99 per cent of people are friendly and helpful because we are all in the same situation. We swap stories about the food – it's vegetarian and simple because the country is so poor – and exchange snacks. No one is a dick on the trail in terms of pushing past or not letting you through. People are considerate – kind, even. It's the best of humanity.

I ask Suman if he's noticed any differences since he started doing the trail, and he said one big change, in that there are more Chinese trekkers than ever before.

I meet a Chinese couple fairly early on in my trek who are trapped in their language because they don't speak English.

At first, we see them fiddling with their phone; they have trouble getting Wi–Fi to power their translation app. They don't have a guide or a porter and since the guide is the one who negotiates your accommodation and sorts out your meals, they are in trouble.

Some of the lodge staff and Suman are laughing at them and their confusion and inability to understand things. It makes me feel uncomfortable.

But then, the world widens a tiny crack. It turns out they are looking for a porter and someone helps them with a mixture of broken English and hand gestures. A couple of days later, we see them on the track and say hello. They break into a smile.

A couple of days after that, while walking down a track I hear the loveliest baritone voice singing opera, and it turns out to be the Chinese man as he clomps down the stairs with gusto. I smile at him and his wife as they pass by.

'You're strong!' she says to me and mimes Arnold Schwarzenegger pumping his biceps. She earns my life-long devotion.

A day after that, we see them at a restaurant, and the Chinese lady comes up to me and gestures for help with her translation app. I'm kind of pleased she picked me to help her.

She points at what I am eating – vegetable noodle soup, holding my steaming bowl with two eggs floating in the broth. The woman nods and taps it into the phone and shows me what it says so she can show it to the waiter.

My heart sinks.

'Ah, no,' I reply. 'That reads "vegetable faces".'

She taps some more. It reads 'egg faces'. These guys are going to be eating next week at this rate.

~

The last and most epic stretch is the day's walk to base camp. The landscape changes entirely, as if shrugging off a shawl to reveal the bare skin beneath, a glimpse of the heartbeat.

The path cuts away to a valley, a long, flat path laid between rows of mountains.

They are like sentinels, the tallest peaks dissolving into a vast, curling cloud of steam at the top. Some of their surfaces are covered in a carpet of moss, some beginning new life from the snow melt, others dying and turning copper. We walk on long, yellow grass, and when the sun frees itself from the cloud, we are in a corridor of gold.

It's a forgotten land, a different realm. This is the healing hum of the earth, not cities, where we think our own noise is the only one worth listening to. Once through the valley we walk a narrow path hemmed in by slabs of rock. Next to us is a glacial stream, and to our left rises a huge wall of snow caps.

The trail gets quieter and quieter as we go along. Not everyone makes it to base camp, and some make it in their own time, so I don't pass anyone for a time. The sky drains into white, clouds cloak the mountains and, soon, snow starts falling.

As we walk, everything is so obscured and ethereal it feels like I'm walking through a mist of creation.

At base camp, everything is hushed, the landscape hidden, and the dining room starts filling up with people. You can't light fires after a certain altitude on the ABC circuit, so it gets cold and wet. The room is packed and feels like a warren filled with rabbits, tired and close together for body warmth. Most of us are staying in dorms, so when it's time to go to bed, we all stream out of the dining room and settle in for more rabbit warmth.

When first light hits, I get up to use the bathroom, but what I see stops me in my tracks. The sky is clear, and the mist and the clouds have departed to reveal the most staggering sight I have seen: snow caps so close I can almost smell their breath of frost and ice. The Annapurna range stretches her long body into the distance, peak after peak, speckled with white against sharp crags. She is so austere and beautiful, and the close knit of mountains seals off the track so dramatically, she feels like the full stop to this part of the earth.

Thick snow covers everything, and in the half-bluish light, a black mountain dog pads over for a bit of attention.

I know that in a matter of minutes, people will start waking up. So I take the time to look at her, truly look at her, and think about how this feels.

I feel the frequency of true silence as I walk through the snow. It is the most beautiful sound I have ever heard – not empty, not lonely at all.

When the sunrise meets the point of earth nearest to me, I'm surrounded by mountains which seem as if they are on fire. The peaks are the colour of flame and slowly the light consumes me until I'm standing there, with tears in my eyes.

Getting here wasn't easy.

Barring hardcore farmer and fisher people, most South Asians are utterly shit at the outdoors. We wear suede boots in muddy fields, carry chiffon shawls in freezing temperatures, ballet pumps on snowy terrain. We can barely inch out the corkscrew from a Swiss Army knife, let alone use it in any meaningful way.

I think back to what I've experienced on the ABC. I've slipped on ice, my knees issued a strongly worded 'fuck you' to my brain, I kept going through valleys of golden grass, thickets of bamboo, beech trees drunk on sunlight, tiny ferns, steps disguised as boulders. I saw a moon shaped like a scythe. I met people, I made friends and heard their stories and shared mine. For a short time I stopped connecting with people from behind a wall of technology and I started connecting with them using my eyes, heart and brain.

I know I'm not unique or that I've even done anything that registers on the scale of impressive things to do. I know that as we speak someone is trudging through Antarctica or travelling around the world in a kayak. I know I'm not Cheryl Strayed, that I didn't grow up with the outdoors, that I can't put up a tent, light a fire or pull off a toenail.

But I brought my heart along with me. This heart that

has been through so much. This heart which is so full of Rob and the past; this heart that struggles with the future.

I place my heart at the feet of mountains and ask for strength and the courage to know my own mind that has been shattered in the past two years.

And, as always when I am in the centre of a silent and calm place, I say to him who is now of sky and earth: 'I hope, wherever you are, there is peace, and there is laughter.'

8

THE CALL TO WEIGH ANCHOR

I have an odd memory from when I was very little in India. Like most kid memories, it is painted in bright, vivid colours but can only be recounted in snatches – there are gaps of information such as: where we were going, who I was with. It's like watching a short film but with deleted scenes.

In this memory, we are driving to someone's house in another state. We decide to stop at a small town to use the loo and grab a bite to eat, and this place is dusty and quiet. There is only one thing to see here: an anatomy museum.

The museum is empty, and to my child brain, it is vast in size. We walk down long aisles and it's the first time I see organs pickled in fluid. There are jars upon jars for the smaller body parts – animal and human – and there's even a series of cases showing the preserved remains of babies at different stages of life.

At the time, it didn't seem creepy or unusual that we were there.

When I returned to Bangalore after Nepal, I felt like parts

of me had been removed and placed in those jars of yellow fluid. Somewhere, pieces of myself were sitting in a dusty, timeless town for the time being, while I was reconfiguring my sense of self.

I already felt different. For the first time, I didn't feel like I belonged anywhere. It wasn't sad or lonely, it was just life and me working out how to be with each other.

It began the moment I stepped off the plane. I felt the warm, gentle mood of the air. I closed my eyes and pressed my thoughts to the further reaches of the city, coconut trees, old buildings mouldy with rain, cars, rickshaws puttering past, buses with 'OK horn please' painted on their backs, and I felt its familiarity unfolding around me.

As my taxi pushed through the slog of the city's traffic, I saw familiar landmarks.

One of them was the Chris Hospital. Whenever we drove past this, Mum and I joked about it – as it's named after Christ.

'You can't just abbreviate the son of God's name to Chris. Like, "Yo, what's up, Chris?"!'

She cackled with laughter. I thought of my parents, and the smiles on their faces when I'd arrive at the gates. Dad had cried, apparently, when he learned that I had made it safely and hadn't been eaten by mountain lions in Nepal. (There are no mountain lions in Nepal, but such a detail is irrelevant to he who worries.)

I thought of my little mum with her dazzling smile and curly hair. I don't know what made me do it, but I thought of the day when they wouldn't be around and my heart almost stopped there and then.

The reason this felt strange was that, in all my life, I have never been the one who left. Since I was a kid, people have been leaving me like shoals of fish pulsing towards more exciting waters, returning after a time.

When we were small kids, Priya and I lived in different countries, then we were separated from Dad during our five-year stint in India. When we were older, Priya had various periods living in America, India and France, while our parents spent half of the year abroad travelling.

I couldn't shake the worry of: what if something happened to them while I was away?

And then, I realise, this is the fear that I've carried all along. I couldn't do anything about people leaving, but if I was the one who stayed, then I'd be there when they decided to come back. Really, this constant anger I have felt since Rob's passing is actually me being scared of losing them.

But I don't think I can live like that any more. I have to see what it is like to be the one who leaves, who makes decisions for herself rather than holding so tightly onto everything.

I don't belong in India, but I don't belong anywhere else either – not for the time being. When I reach back for my sense of belonging, my anchor to England, it is not there. Someone has pulled it up from the bottom of the sea.

We have a few days together before I move on to New

Zealand. Dad is going to stay on a little longer to get in as much sunshine as possible, but Mum's decided she wants to get back to her home in England and get things set up.

When I hug Mum goodbye, and I feel how small she is, I almost start crying. It's as if the moment of when I will never touch or smell her again has been briefly brought forward, and the loss of her, an inevitable future without her, is a sensation so sharp I can't bear it.

She gives us instructions on where to find things, what tasks she needs us to do. I look at my dad doubtfully – he has big shoes to fill in her absence. He gives me the same look.

I see for the first time how lost we will be without her, how she makes our life easier through tireless effort and cajoling. We are dumbasses moving through the dark by dint of her light.

After I say goodnight to her, I hear her moving about in the next room. I don't want to let her go. I run out of my room and throw my arms around her. She looks up at me, this tiny, beautiful, strong brown woman who has been through so much, the little dynamo in our lives. She knows, without saying a word, that I am smelling our mortality.

She says with infinite love and patience, 'Remember I am always with you.'

Then she holds my face and looks at me. 'And when you go to New Zealand, say hello to Rob from me.'

~

I swear this isn't *Eat, Pray, Love*, but I'm going to talk about belief again.

Nothing much had changed with God and me since the temple experience in Nepal, but it did get me thinking about how I fit in with the world. What did I believe? What was my own philosophy about life?

I still didn't believe 'everything happens for a reason' – a belief that collapses quickly under the weight of things such as Ebola and Justin Bieber.

But what had begun in Nepal was a strengthening of the self, met with the bigger question: what gives my life meaning? And when thinking about the future: what do I want to give me meaning?

The epiphany came when, a few days before we parted ways, Mum, Dad and I drove to Pondicherry in the neighbouring state of Tamil Nadu. It's a union territory because it was formed out of four French colonial enclaves.

Pondi, as we call it, was a place we visited when we were children. My main memory was that of the seafront promenade, pretty colonial buildings and French shutters.

As we drive through, there's a dichotomy between the Indian part and what's called 'White Town', where the French used to stay. Surprise, surprise, the Indian part is more haphazard and dirty, while White Town has broad streets and more money.

Walking around, you see pastel-coloured buildings

emerging between rain trees and white pillars blackened by monsoons of the past.

Beyond the quaint colonialisms, Pondi is also a place where two big spiritual leaders lived – Sri Aurobindo and his spiritual collaborator, a French woman named Mirra Alfassa.

Aurobindo was a wise man originally from Bengal, who died in 1950 aged seventy-eight; Mirra Alfassa died in her nineties in the '70s. Together, they held and discussed huge discourses on philosophy, and their teachings have now been distilled into books. When we arrive, we decide we want to go and visit Auroville, which is their centre of learning and houses an impressive building called the Matrimandir – or Mother's Temple.

But it's not really a temple, and the beliefs of Aurobindo and Mirra Alfassa were non-denominational. The building itself is a short walk from the gates of Auroville, and it is like something from science fiction.

A vast, golden dome made from beaten steel panels covered with gold leaf, it looks like a temporarily parked spaceship. Inside, there are various points to meditate and it has been designed so that a special crystal in the centre of the building channels light from the sun and pings it around the room.

At first, there's something undeniably cult-y about it. Mirra Alfassa is referred to as the Mother. There are photos of them everywhere. Then there is the Matrimandir itself, its futuristic shape and feel, not to mention the mega crystal.

Hippies roam around the grounds, mixed in with Indian tourists taking selfies on their iPhones. Finally, there are set rules – if you want to visit the Matrimandir, you have to sit in a room and watch a video first.

It is a surreal sight: Mum, Dad and me sitting in the smallish room, watching a video while the soothing, flat voiceover washes over us. I mean, if I was going to try to brainwash someone, that's the voice I'd use.

But the thing is, it's not a cult. And I'm not saying that because I'm now in the cult.

I'm almost ashamed of my cynicism by the end of it. What I find out, both from the videos and the museum that reveals all of the architectural secrets of the Matrimandir, is that their teachings, coupled with how I've been feeling inside, knits together a philosophy I've been drawn to for a while now.

Basically, it's about the internal self – so shoring up and making yourself feel as strong, balanced and loving as you possibly can be. To seek those answers within, rather than looking for something external to fix your unhappiness or dissatisfaction with life. They are big believers in meditation but, interestingly, it's not a fixed type of meditation – they call it concentration. So it's just finding a spot and being quiet for a while.

There's a moment when we enter a meditation spot and I say sternly to Dad, who doesn't have a clue about medi-tation and I just KNOW he's going to clonk in there with his general observations, 'Dad, you have to be quiet, no interruptions, okay?' Mum and I sit, and we take in the peace and calm, the freshness of the air and the gardens, but he can't help himself. 'Hey, look at that guy's funny shirt.'

We both glare at him.

Really, what Auroville was and is supposed to be is a place where people can come together above all of the things that cause disagreement such as race and politics.

It was dreamed of as a city of the future, a living embodiment of human unity and somewhere that could harness the best of humanity. It didn't quite achieve that, but it still has a strong community and visitors come from all over the world to see it.

For it to connect with someone spiritually sceptical like me, as a place where people can just come and rest, and be still and quiet, with no hidden agenda, that's impressive.

I had one last niggle which was the reference to the divine, but when I looked it up it said the divine is 'all the knowledge we have to acquire, all the power we have to obtain, all the love we have to become'. So, not a bearded man sitting on a cloud.

It also starts me thinking about a different sense of purpose.

There is and always will be a huge hole left behind by Rob. I don't think I will ever fill it by stuffing more things into the gap. But perhaps I've been pulling away from people in anger, when the solution actually lies within them.

There are slabs of stone with quotes from the Mother lining the way to the Matrimandir building, and there is one that stays with me for a while.

'Do not think of who you have been, think only of who you want to be and you are sure to progress.'

It gives me a lot to think about after I say goodbye to my parents and embark on one final journey before leaving India.

~

Most of my family live in Bangalore, but some are scattered across America, England and the rest of India. Very few of us live in Mangalore – the place we are originally from.

For a sense of where it is, hover above Bangalore on the map of India and draw your eyes west.

It is the largest port city in the state of Karnataka, a place held by the Arabian Sea and the mountainous Western Ghats. Although Mangalore hums with construction work, imported cars and technology now, back when I was a child it used to be a hot, humid swamp town.

Mum and I arrived in 1987 to stay with her parents; Priya was already living with them by that time. Dad was intending to join us once he had sold our house in England.

I left the quiet of our Kent house and my little tidy room of books and carpeting, for Mangalore's tamarind fish curries, blaring noise and mosquitoes. Her minimum level of humidity is 50 per cent; when she's feeling vengeful, it's 93.

My younger self can't remember much of her beyond sandstone walls and coconut trees, dust and heat, the rain working the reddish mud up into thick rivers flowing down culverts.

I was too involved in the cultural disconnect between India and England: one had electricity, the other had temperamental moods around electricity; one had comfortable duvets and loo paper, the other had thin sheets and a bum bucket.

It has been twenty-five years since I have visited. This time round, though, I have a better understanding about belonging. Apart from when I went to a specific community event of our people in England, I have never, ever bumped into another Shetty.

I thought the characteristics that marked my family were unique to my family; I never imagined that they marked an actual place. I hear people speaking our language – Tulu – in the street, at the supermarket. Before, it had only ever really been in people's living rooms. They are polite, don't barge into you and are well-spoken. 'Dignified' is the most apt word.

Mangalore, when viewed from a distance, is what a city looks like before it has been swallowed whole by steel, concrete and glass. Buildings, lights and phone masts crop up from within the dense knit of coconut trees, and it still retains its sense of greenery and poise.

It is already too late for Bangalore, which, like every other city, wrought a Faustian deal and traded identity for money and cheap tech, but Mangalore's soul is still here.

Around a 45-minute drive from the city is Mulki, a stretch of land that fringes the backwaters of Mangalore. We never visited it as kids, and I'd never heard of it until now.

Its quiet existence is why it remains the beautiful, peaceful place it is today. Everyone has heard of the backwaters in Kerala, but this is a glimpse of what Kerala may have looked like before she had boats chugging diesel up and down Lake Vembanad.

Through a leafy curtain of coconut trees, the river lies further ahead. A kingfisher zips past and marks our arrival; a brahminy kite looks balefully at us with a *you're not fish* stare.

My reason for coming here is the Mantra Surf Club. Surfing is a relatively new concept in India compared with the rest of the world. Mangalore's beaches, like other parts of the Indian coastline, are notoriously deceptive.

They draw you in with their untouched beauty, but the waters are fast, treacherous and their currents will suck the life from your bones if you aren't careful. However, in this particular spot, there is a protected part of coast that creates waves just right for beginners.

Mantra is special because it doesn't just teach tourists to surf, it also encourages surfing in the local community, especially girls. Indians – especially Indian women – aren't encouraged to do activities in the water because you get dark in the sun.

I love that there is a cool little organisation that sticks two fingers up to the norms and arranges surfing in the morning, paddleboarding or kayaking in the evening.

The river here is quiet and flat, thoughtful. Along her right flank, she stretches towards a curve, framed in tiny stubs of mangroves. The day before I begin my surfing lessons, I go kayaking and pitch my canoe into the water, under a swirl of kites beadily watching the water below. Tiny fish arc across the water to escape to another part of the river, silver bolts of lightning where the light catches them.

As the sun begins its descent, a fiery smudge in the corner of my eyes, the water gathers weight; it becomes heavy, denser, like it's holding all of itself in, in preparation for the darkness to come.

As my paddle dips in, it feels thicker, like it is calling to some quietness within the water. And it is quiet, so quiet, and you get the sense that although lives are ticking away along the riverbank – maybe someone is washing clothes, or another person is gutting fish for the evening meal – it is hidden away from sight.

I close my eyes and there's a line, a rope to the landscape, a feeling, a heartbeat.

There is something utterly different when you are in the place that built the skin and bones of your ancestors, a clicking together of pieces. Is this what other people feel like when they are home?

Do they even notice that subtle settling down of the shoulders, an unspoken language between their own history and the landscape? Even if I will never live here, this is a moment that I can fashion into belonging and peace and take with me wherever I go.

Yet I know, if I had grown up here, if I did live here, that I wouldn't feel like this; I wouldn't have this relationship with the water. I certainly wouldn't have grown up here thinking I could hop on a paddleboard or try surfing, or any of those things. I'd have felt like I couldn't because being in the sun means you get dark, and there's that relentless discourse about the unattractiveness of dark skin.

The next day is surfing, a sport I have only tried once and was utterly terrible at. I'm joined by two Indian men around my age and my shoulders immediately stiffen.

The reason being, I always feel self-conscious about my body in India because the men are far more outright in their staring than in most other parts of the world. Sex and the female body is digested mostly in one of two ways: either in an unrealistic Bollywood film or at home, where women are probably covered up. There's no in between to normalise the female form.

I almost never wear swimwear in India that's revealing, especially after I once saw a group of men in Goa taking pictures of a white tourist's arse as she was sunbathing in a bikini. This sense of shame was drilled into me from such a young age that, quite honestly, I didn't wear a bikini until I was about twenty-eight regardless of where in the world I was.

I'm wearing a long-sleeved rash vest and shorts to surf. We take our boards to the water and, despite my self-consciousness, it turns out I have nothing to worry about. These guys are two days ahead of me in the three-day surfing course, and all they are concerned with is trying to perfect their surf before it's time for them to go home.

While I wait on the beach for my instructor to finish getting them set up, I take in my surroundings.

Along the beach, crabs do their sideways shifty shuffle across hot sand, peeping out from the tip of a tunnel. Some of them are the colour of glass dipped in milk, tiny creatures leading little crustacean lives beneath our thumping feet.

There is no one on the beach, save for the kites circling overhead, the crash of waves fulfilling their promise to return to the shore, the swirl of the river mouth nearby where currents collide and swirl. Nearby are rocks you'd half expect mermaids to perch on while picking remnants of foolish men from their teeth.

When I grew up, like a thousand other brown girls, I always thought of mermaids as having pink skin and red hair, like Ariel in Disney. But here, with the electricity of my homeland coursing through my feet, I imagine the mermaids of India with indigo skin, teeth like pearls and large eyes ringed in coal. Beautiful, dark, deadly. Lost in the foam and waiting just out of reach. I wonder how many hearts they have crunched, how many songs they have sung to lure us to this place of beauty.

I start humming to myself and, after a time, my instructor yells at me to come to the water's edge.

The next few hours are a humiliation, as I launch myself over and over again into the water and manage to stand up on my board a grand total of once.

Further along the shoreline, some of the younger members of Mantra are surfing, and they look effortless, gliding into the water and dancing across their board as the wave catches the underside.

Exhausted, cranky, but pleased with our progress, we head back to the main house where a vegetarian lunch is waiting for us. Ravi and Sanjay, the two guys I went surfing with, don't join us, and, at first, I'm relieved. Even though they don't seem strange, now I don't have to make small talk.

But then we're thrown together in the early evening, as the Wi-Fi only works in the communal lounge space, and are clustered around the one table. I radiate 'don't speak to me' vibes but, undeterred, one of them strikes up a conversation. This is the first time I've had a conversation with two completely strange Indian men, and in a matter of moments, our easy chat and laughter remind me of my male university friends.

We share some stories; they make me laugh. Ravi is in love with a girl whose father disapproves of him and is discussing plans to elope, while Sanjay is divorced and totally cynical about love. The two met in Australia, where they were living at the time, and moved back to New Delhi.

Then, they say, 'Look, we can't hack the 24/7 veggie food here. Do you want to come with us to this restaurant we've been secretly going to?'

Part of me is hesitant, and the other part *carpe diems* and wins. The walk and conversation is easy and comforting, like we've known each other for years. After dinner, we walk back in the dark, our stomachs full of butter chicken and naan. We hear the chirp of insects in the fields and pick our way back by the light of our phones. I feel safe, comfortable, full and happy.

It may not seem like much, but these two have broadened my experience of Indian men, and slowly the world widens and changes its shape. Don't get me wrong – I won't be wearing a bikini anytime soon on an Indian beach, but it makes me think of my preconceptions of India and what I now know.

This India is poised, quiet, patient, waiting.

This India stirs in me something deep. It reaches out its hand and, for the first time in my life, I willingly take it and allow the quiet and familiarity to heal the most grief-torn parts of me.

~

As I pack for New Zealand, a full thirteen hours ahead of most of my loved ones, 18,323km from London, I wonder if I'm going to miss them.

Chris Rock, in his stand-up show *Tamborine* for Netflix, said that it's impossible these days to miss someone. 'You can't miss nobody – not really – you can say it, but you don't really miss them. You are with them all the time, they're in your fucking pocket!'

He's got a point. Technology has completely changed the concept of missing a person. WhatsApp, Facebook and Instagram mean that even though we're not in the same time zone, rarely a day goes by when I don't have contact with my friends or family. I remember how it felt to miss them when I was a child, and whatever the emotion, it is now of a different shape and colour.

I thought I was fixing things by taking myself away from my life, from them. But had I got it wrong? Even if I felt pressure to be or act a certain way, didn't I need them in my life to give it meaning?

In a sweet-yet-terrible romcom film with Richard Gere and Susan Sarandon called *Shall We Dance?*, there's a quote that unexpectedly pierced my heart, which applies to marriage but I think can be applied to all the loves in our lives.

Sarandon says, 'We need a witness to our lives. There's a billion people on the planet, what does any one life really mean? But in a marriage, you're promising to care about everything. The good things, the bad things, the terrible things, the mundane things, all of it, all of the time, every day. You're saying, "Your life will not go unnoticed because I will notice it. Your life will not go unwitnessed because I will be your witness."'

Regardless of whether you are married or you aren't, that act of bearing witness seems to hold the key to loneliness and finding meaning in life. It's not as simple as partying a lot or being constantly surrounded by people. We know as much from high male suicide statistics and men's mental health insight that the man most likely to kill himself most probably has tons of friends.

I was trying to get to the root of how important human connection was in life, and why.

I had started this journey a bit angry, pissed off about the hand I'd been dealt. Rather than work out how I fitted into people's lives, I'd decided I didn't, and therefore I needed to remove myself from that particular life. I did it because I needed time to think, but if I'm being truthful, part of my journey was also about seeking validation for living a remote existence in the future.

People lived in remote spots, and quiet places, so it could be done. But the question was: was my intention about living that kind of specific life or was it about removing myself from people before they had a chance to remove me?

When you're on a boat, and you need to set sail, you have to 'weigh anchor'. That's the term for pulling the anchor up so you can remove what's holding you down and fixing you to that place.

I had made myself weigh anchor, and had begun this journey to seek validation for leading a solitary life because I believed that being around other people was pressuring me into making decisions that weren't my own.

I was so sure I was right that before embarking on the next leg of my journey, I asked Eric Klinenberg, who was basically an expert at being alone, and was so sure that he'd agree with me that, when he didn't, I was rattled.

His observation was that it wasn't possible to be solitary and happy. Being alone is not the same as being solitary and his observation was that a lot of happiness and fulfilment stems from other people.

Relationships really do matter, he told me. He said we

needed not just one type of social support but a lot of different kinds, and some need more of it than others. He also stressed the importance of asking yourself what a meaningful connection looked like to you.

It reminded me of my correspondence with Oliver Burkeman, who said we are organisms who have evolved to benefit from social interactions. At the most basic level, that includes leaving the house to talk to the person who bags your groceries or serves you coffee. Even a small interaction like that can make you feel less isolated. But that has to be underpinned by interacting with people who really know you. Because their understanding of you is a signal to your brain that you are understood and seen, and that is a critical antidote to loneliness.

Being understood, being witnessed – that seemed to be the most important thing to a lot of people. The question is, without Rob, the person who was my witness, how was I supposed to navigate that with friends and family? Or was it a question of recalibrating the level of importance in each relationship?

If I was ill, I could think of three people who know me well enough to come to my sickbed and shout at the nurse for giving me vanilla ice cream. 'SHE LIKES CHOCOLATE AND ONLY CHOCOLATE!'

It might seem like a trivial thing – ice cream – but it meant I was seen, known and understood. It was an anchor to my past, present and future. It meant someone had listened. Someone knew my history of being aggravatingly annoying by studying an entire ice-cream menu only to always ever order the same thing. It may not be mysterious. But as I have come to learn, love is at its most powerful when it is known. When it is built upon the shore of memory, experience and history. It may not be a fire that constantly blazes, but it is a steady, slow warmth nonetheless.

9

THE WORLD'S SECOND BLUEST SKY

When I arrive in New Zealand, the cicadas have already begun. Their hum fills the warm air, and for the first time in my life, I see the pohutukawas blossoming against the blue summer sky.

I pick up a crimson bloom from the pavement and turn it over in my hand. Fine red dust scatters over my fingertips. There are trees on almost every avenue, branches fanning out from their sturdy trunks, shaking out their skirts of tightly bunched bright-red flowers.

They only bloom in December and January and are known as New Zealand's Christmas tree because of the time of year. Every Kiwi speaks of them with fondness, and their ability to grow in the hardiest of conditions means they sometimes pop up where you least expect them.

They can live for a thousand years, hold their own against winds, brutal Southern sea spray and drought. If ever a tree could represent a nation's ability to endure and the beauty that lies within its endurance, this is it.

The pohutukawas mean something else: their blossoming marks the start of the longest time I will ever spend in New Zealand. There is a different shape and scent to this visit; it isn't so steeped in grief. When I visited two years ago, it was very much a yearning for Rob. I had flown over for the funeral but it was so brief, so wrought in the fire of mourning, that while I was saying goodbye to him, I wasn't able to say goodbye to the land.

My return, then, was a desperate need to be in the place he was in before he died. I wanted New Zealand's seas to calm the storm. I wanted her to wash away some of the guilt and regret and tell me it was okay. It was also the place where I felt I could talk about him regularly because I was with his family, and the hurt was deeper here.

But this trip, nearly three years after Rob passed, was my heart saying to my in-laws: there is something more than this now. We're not just clinging to each other in grief. We are actively choosing each other.

Although this trip wasn't about grief, there is a dull ache in the days approaching Christmas, as there always is. Each year it lessens, but the advent of Rob's birthday on 23 December, followed by Christmas and then New Year, always feels heavier.

I always miss him, but this – as with his death anniversary – is more acute. Though as I discover in New Zealand, the feeling is no worse than it was last year; I've just learned to recognise it for what it is: a heavy time in which I need to pay extra attention to how I feel and what I'm comfortable doing.

Around this time, I have a few tough conversations with some of my loved ones back home. It turns out a few people were concerned about me coming to New Zealand in case it made things harder.

I want to say, gently, 'Nothing makes it harder. It is hard, period. If I am getting up, socialising, going to work, then, trust me, I'm doing enough. Whatever I need to do to try to heal myself, I'm going to try.

'Staying in London, or staying in one place doesn't make it easier. My sadness is still there. I have been indifferent about being alive when I've had my closest friends and family around me. So everything is worth trying.'

A few days after I arrive, I go alone to the cemetery on Rob's birthday. I know I will be coming back a couple of days later on Christmas Day with Prue and David, and I want this moment to myself.

It's the first time I'll be seeing his headstone, and when I get there, I see a lot of cars parked up. A closer look reveals two small marquees in the cemetery and people are eating.

I'm flummoxed. Did someone die and sandwiches were required immediately after the ceremony because a large number of them were hypoglycaemic?

When I tell David afterwards, he says, 'Was it on the grass near the exit?'

He was referring to a broad patch of clear space that might pass for a small park if you weren't in a cemetery. 'No,' I replied. 'Like literally they could've used a headstone to rest their coffee cups on.' We both shook our heads and agreed it was weird.

Thankfully, they aren't anywhere near Rob's grave, and when I approach the headstone, my breath catches in my mouth. It is really real. This really happened. He's not waiting for me back home. *Will I ever stop feeling like he's waiting for me back home?* I wonder.

Forever In Our Hearts
Robert Owen Bell
Beloved Husband of Poorna
Dearly Loved Son of Prue and David
Brother of John and Alan
Treasured Friend

I run my fingers over his name and my name.

I think of him beneath my feet, and that half of my soul is wrapped around him, keeping him company. As always here, my heart swells with the thought of him.

If I close my eyes, your every movement is a calling song. Your sigh, the rustle of your book, the smooth slip of your T-shirt over your head. I can feel the fuzzy close shave of your hair as my hand rubs over it, the curve of where your bottom lip meets mine as I kiss you to sleep.

The muscle memory of you is the meeting point between haunting and comfort.

I love lists, and when I think of Rob, sometimes I name the things we used to buy in the supermarket or dishes only he knew how to make. Or I think of moments only we shared, such as him coming to meet me at the train station after work with Daisy bounding around scaring the shit out of the other passengers while we said our hellos with a kiss.

The memories of our departed ones are held most powerfully in the moments that made them human, that made them unique in our lives, no matter how mundane it may have seemed at the time.

My Rob Bell shopping list on his birthday is:

- Huge, oversized pasta
- Pork meatballs à la Rob
- Oranges (the big ones)
- Sensodyne toothpaste
- Israeli couscous and feta salad
- Bakers dog biscuits
- Lucozade
- Squeaky toys from the £1 shop

Anniversaries are tough after someone dies because they are the chain connecting your past together and your present alone. I have a friend who says forgetting anniversaries is a good thing because it means you've moved on, but I don't agree.

I think humans by their very nature prefer to forget; it's a rare person who sharpens their pain daily on a whetstone and marinates in the misery. But remembering is important; it is release.

Anniversaries are the moment when all the universes of your loss converge together and allow you to freefall into the memory of them. You give yourself permission to experience the intensity of the sweetness and sorrow that it creates, that maybe you don't in your daily life.

He would have been forty-two. I wonder what our lives would have been like. Would we have gotten back together? Fleetingly, I touch my hand to my stomach, the ghost action of a baby that would never come, not from him, anyway.

I think about the idea I have been pushing away for weeks since I turned thirty-seven a couple of months previously.

What was I going to do about having kids?

~

Here's what I think I know about people and kids.

If you don't have them, when someone you know has them, there's a place they have gone to that you can't go to, yet. You can't even pretend this is a place you've visited, or perhaps you popped your head in the window – it's a place so primordial, so heavy and raw, pulsing with life, blood and light.

Grief changes a person, but creating life changes a person too. It literally changes your body if you are a woman and, internally, unpicks every lock to every room inside you and rearranges the contents.

If you are a mother, you are the human equivalent of a female werewolf – strong, powerful and capable of transformation between that wild place where you created your baby, and the calm, serene space where you will raise it.

Afterwards, you struggle between your selves. Between maintaining a balance, feeling the new person you are, groping around for the parts of you from before.

Motherhood, to me, starts like a siren song. There's a tug in your belly, an urge that presses a switch that overrides everything else. I know, because I felt it. Not very often, and very late in life compared to other people, but I felt that yearning, that every single part of me was unfurling, petal by petal, to give another little person a chance at life.

I first felt that tug when Leela was born. It was indescribable, the love I felt for her. It wasn't jealousy or regret, and at that moment Rob was alive and standing opposite me in the hospital room. As we gathered around my beautiful niece, it was the biggest glow I had ever experienced.

But I also knew, as that tug began, that it wasn't as simple as Rob and I having children. I knew he was in trouble with his drinking around that time, and two weeks after that hospital visit Rob had a terrible relapse on alcohol and was self-harming. He then went into a hospital of a very different kind: a psychiatric hospital.

Whatever was going on with him and us, we couldn't have children at that point. It was too chaotic; his recovery was in its infancy. Mentally I was also shutting down and expending any extra energy on dealing with Rob and the situation I had found myself in. When we separated, I knew that even if we got back together, kids were not going to be a possibility for us.

We may have breathed them momentarily into existence when we spoke about having them, when we imagined what they would look like and who they would become. We may have loved these little ghost children as deeply as we loved each other and the promise of the future they held, but we also both knew we could never bring an innocent life into the chaos of addiction.

When he died, in addition to the many strands of grief my life had become, I grieved the loss of our children. But it's a grief I would have had to have undergone even if he was still alive. Because that's what grief is: it's saying good-bye to your past, present and future regardless of whether death is in the equation or not.

There are so many people who are dealing with a miscarriage, the loss of a child who died before they had the chance to be a child.

The couple who desperately want children but cannot have them, made to deal with their loss privately, and forced to volley questions from other people about when they're going to have kids. Or perhaps the single man or woman who doesn't want to have kids by themselves and has reached an age where it's time to say goodbye to the dream of it all.

All of that is grief; all of that is loss.

At thirty-seven, there is a hard mathematics I have to deal with that I didn't have to when I was in my early thirties.

If I want kids, I have to start thinking about it now. I don't have endless amounts of time. And although I would never want to relive my twenties, fun as they were, there is a sharp pang of longing for that decade which is so soaked in time, so fat with possibilities.

First, I needed to acknowledge that I'd be doing it on my own. In terms of time, I didn't have the luxury of waiting for a long-term relationship that may never happen, and I have never been the person to be romantically involved with someone to facilitate a goal.

When I fall for someone, it's a wild, thick bramble that grows fast and quick; it's unexpected and intense. I could never imagine being with someone because I had a hidden agenda. I knew that I was lucky to have experienced the love of a person like Rob in a lifetime. To expect it to happen twice would be like a greedy child gorging on sweet strawberries.

So what did that mean for me as a mother-in-waiting?

I was drawn to unconventional stories of motherhood. My friend and agent Rowan, who had been single for a while, had decided to have a baby through a donor.

When we met for coffee – she beautiful and pregnant, me fascinated with her will and determination – she told me that she had reached a point where she wanted to have a child, and realised that, because of her age, she'd rather do it on her own than wait for a relationship to facilitate it. It doesn't mean she's given up on dating or a relationship, rather that motherhood was immensely important to her, and all of that other stuff could come after she'd had her baby.

I remember at the time feeling hope. Where once that door had seemed shut, it now opened a crack. But I also wasn't sure whether I had it in me to physically have a baby on my own. I didn't know if I wanted it as much.

I was telling Has about this on the phone and she said, 'Well, look at Sushmita Sen.'

'What about her?' I asked. Sushmita Sen was a Bollywood actress who was really big when we were kids. She won Miss Universe when I was fourteen, and I remember it being a big deal that an Indian woman had won it. She hadn't done a huge amount of high-profile stuff for a while, though – at least nothing that had come across my radar, because I wasn't a huge Hindi film buff.

'She adopted her oldest daughter when she was twenty-four, and then adopted another girl a while after that. And she's this single mother fitness guru,' she said.

I grabbed my phone and looked her up on Instagram. I had a thousand questions. I had always loved the idea of adoption even if I'd had my own children, and here was this forty-something Indian woman who had decided at a young age that she wanted to be a mother. It wasn't easy for single mothers to adopt, and she'd done it not once but twice, and without nannies.

When I thought of the parents I most wanted to be like if I did become a mother, they were people who were most honest about parenthood. Above all, they were still themselves, and still safeguarded that part of them that wasn't fused to a child. It acted as a second brain, allowing them to think about their choices and dreams, not just their child's choices and dreams.

And I knew that as much as it was joyous and a feeling unlike any other, it was also tough. I knew my niece was a beauty; a well-behaved, clever child more so than the average. But I also knew she had sick days, and days when, however cute she was, she could be a little ratbag, as all children are. Priya had Shabby, who is a father extraordinaire. Mum and I are continually amazed at his endless reservoir of patience when it comes to Leela. To not have someone to support you through those days – to have to deal with everything: potty training, food prep, nappy changing – it seemed like a lot.

But I also saw the look that bloomed on my sister's face when Leela was just being Leela – saying something funny or being affectionate. Priya's entire countenance changed, as if she remembered her spark of creation, and all the wishes and dreams she poured into this child she had wanted so much, and now here she was, calling her the most powerful name in existence: Mama.

Do I want a child because I want to feel like that about someone, or do I want a child because I feel, above and beyond, one of my life's purposes is to be a mother?

That muddled feeling leaves me unsure of what my motivations are. It tugs not only on my concerns around my biological clock, but an unwanted memory that has probably shaped me more than I realise.

~

We were ten, my friend Vishnu and I. Mum, Priya and myself were living in a sweet and small flat in Bangalore, right in the centre of town, while Dad was still back in England trying to sell our home in the midst of the recession.

Vishnu's dad worked for the Brooke Bond tea company and they lived in the big house opposite our apartment block, separated by an empty plot of land awaiting commands of construction. We could see each other if we timed it right – me from my balcony on the second floor, him on his parents' balcony standing above a wall of pink bougainvillea.

Although we were in the middle of the city, our homes sat on a quiet, undeveloped side road. A mere five minutes out onto the main street would take you into the blast of rickshaw horns and vendors trundling along with wooden tables selling vegetables, fruit and collecting old newspapers.

But the dirt road was our domain. We bent it to our will by playing hopscotch and hide-and-seek, riding our bikes fearlessly up and down.

We didn't have satellite TV, iPads, video games or smart-phones back then, so entertainment was in the form of comic books and playing with your friends.

Vishnu's mother worked, as did mine.

So we went out to play, a lot. When the monsoon came down, we played indoor games. And when the sun came out and wasn't scorching hot, it was back to exploring the building site or kicking our ball around.

We had the run of the place, but there was one place we knew not to go. It sat at the end of the lane, shrouded in darkness. You knew that if you accidentally kicked a ball into the yard, you'd make a sign of the cross and say your goodbyes to it.

This house had a sad, empty feel about it, as if it had shown up thirty years ago, and nature had forgotten it was there.

Any plants that grew had done so through the school of hard knocks; an evolution that had arrived at the hands of hard Indian summers and the relentless rains. The leaves dark and sour, anything flowering long since fled for kinder turf.

It belonged to a forty-something lady named Ms D'Costa. She wasn't seen very often, but when she emerged, her long, thin, brown body moved across the yard like a wraith as if checking the world was still turning outside her front door.

She definitely didn't seem to like people very much. And when she was seen outside, she seemed tired, as if the dust had crawled in and made a home of her, filling her with emptiness where a life should be.

She hated it when our balls landed in her yard, and sometimes kept them like prisoners who had committed the crime of trespass. If she released them, she almost always did so begrudgingly and through a gust of sharp and prickly words. We'd argue whose fault it was that the ball was kicked into the yard and the loser had to dart in and collect it without being detected.

Rumours abounded about Ms D'Costa because she lived on her own and didn't have children. Maybe she looked after an elderly, incontinent parent in there. Perhaps she used to be married but her husband died. Or she killed him.

If you got too near to her house, the darkness of her home would snake around your ankles and pull you in and you would never be seen again.

There was something not quite right with her, people said, because wasn't it weird that a woman of her age lived on her own? And didn't have kids?

Although we didn't see Ms D'Costa a lot, from time to time, as I got older, she would creep into the edges of my thoughts. The sense that we had got it wrong about her.

What had happened to her life to make her like that? Was it just that she actually had a tragic past or that she had become a reflection of the emptiness in which society saw her – no husband and no kids?

Did she struggle with a mental illness like depression and that's why her curtains were always drawn and she rarely left home? When I think about it, she always seemed tired and sad, rather than angry.

All I know is that no one bothered to ask. Her otherness made her an object of fear and strangeness, and rather than asking about her life, people avoided her.

'You cannot be what you cannot see,' the saying goes, and all my life, single, older women were spoken about in pitying tones, as if they lived a half-life and were permanently doomed to carry around their unhappiness.

In twenty-seven years, I've never really stopped thinking about her. Or any of those other women. Maybe it's because somewhere, deep down inside, I have always worried about turning into them.

~

Christmas comes and goes, peacefully. It's my first Kiwi Christmas, and I don't miss the cold.

'But does it *feel* like Christmas?' my mum asks on the phone.

Ever the smartarse, I reply, 'Do you mean is my stomach bloated with overeating and am I drinking to compensate for the fact that it's dark and miserable? Then, no. Because it's warm and sunny. And it's better, in some ways.'

While I'm here, I'm staying at Felicity's house again, and we fall into our little routine. Felicity is very passionate about interior design and every so often I'll come back and find the furniture rearranged or the art moved about.

Felicity walks her dog Finbar in the morning, while I take to the gym or go for a run. Then we have a brief chat about our day, might reconvene for a drink around 5pm on the sunny wooden deck and have an early night.

At Christmas, we have sixteen people over, but it isn't stressful. Everyone is meant to bring a dish, and that cuts down on the pressure placed on one person to cook. There is salmon cured in gin-soaked beetroot, celeriac puree, crab tartlets, salmon dip, thick slices of bread, potato salad, and of course the Christmas ham.

Prue and David have a new miniature dachshund puppy named Monty, a ball of black and tan fluff who terrorises Finbar while we pile our plates high.

After everyone leaves, it is Felicity, her sister Gabrielle and me left. 'Let's go get trousered,' Felicity says, and we grab beer and red wine.

We sit in the garden and close our eyes against the sun. I hear the lovely lilt of Gabrielle's voice as we talk and cackle, the noises of Felicity pottering about. The air is calm, and Rob is gone but not forgotten.

I'm happy to be here, with the embrace of this family, my family, around me. In two days, I'm going on holiday with Prue, David, Rob's brother John and his girlfriend Sam.

~

The Bay of Islands is renowned for its beauty – lush green rocks emerge from turquoise blues and aquamarines, narrow strips of land peel off from the edge and dive into the sea, ringed in gold sand.

Like most of New Zealand's sights, there is more to her than meets the eye: she is actually a drowned river valley, hence her unusual shape.

This part of the North Island is known for its long, sunny days, which is why so many people come here to retire. A drive through the area unravels fruit orchard after fruit orchard. If the sky seems bluest here, that's because it is.

A researcher back in 2006 measured the levels of colour in the sky using a special portable spectrometer devised by physicists, and found that it has the bluest sky after Rio de Janeiro.

Sun-drenched days and signs for blueberries and fresh ice cream can make it seem impossible to imagine anything bad happening here. It's the place of idyllic childhoods and lazy afternoons, swims off the pier and running your hand through water so pure it looks like it trickled through from paradise.

But talk to a Kiwi and you'll hear how economically depressed the area is. Stories of 'P addicts' – addicts to methamphetamine – surface. Addiction to the drug is high in this area, and the impact on kids in surrounding schools is awful – children from chaotic homes often arrive without a packed lunch.

I think about this as Prue and I later find ourselves picking vegetables and fruit in the garden. John and Sam are arriving the next day. David is on the computer. We're all staying in a house that belongs to friends of theirs who are keen gardeners and have spent a lot of love, time and money cultivating their own produce.

In the warm and still summer air, we talk and prod strawberries for their ripeness. I put one in my mouth and through the sweetness I taste the echo of where it was once connected to earth. We find silver beet and cherry tomatoes.

Carrying our haul back to the house, I put my vegetable basket down on the table and pour the two of us a glass of cold white wine. I talk to my mother-in-law about our plans for the next few days. My father-in-law tells us bits of the news as he reads it online.

It is sleepy, quiet, familiar. The warmth of the house makes me doze off; I feel safe and loved.

It seems unthinkable that in four weeks, I'll go through one of the strangest, most unsettling two days of my life, where I am convinced I will die.

10

IN SEARCH OF SILENCE

It is always easier to long for something that is the best version of itself because it never happened.

When I miss Rob, or I mourn the loss of what we never had, such as having children, I'm missing the dream, not the reality. When I miss being in a relationship with him and being loved, what I am thinking of is the most heightened parts of those emotions – the elation, the happiness, the safety – not feeling alone, let down or disappointed.

If I trace a fingertip from this loss of an idealised life back to my present day, the question I overwhelmingly want an answer to is: will I ever be happy?

I think I am asking the wrong question. Of course I have been happy. I was happy when I lay in the sun. Happy when I was laughing at a joke Felicity made when we were discussing life and the universe on her deck. Happy when I thought about my calm little flat and how I'd worked so hard to get it.

Happiness is a positive emotion, so it sounds counter-intuitive to say this – because surely everyone wants to be happy – but there is a problem with it being set as the ultimate goal in life. We now have happiness experts dedicated to telling us how to be happy, a state we desperately crave because we think it will solve our problems.

All it does is create a permanent emotional hunger. We look at people's social media accounts and see them leading happy lives. We tell ourselves that if only we had a body that looked like that person, or if we had a gorgeous partner, then we'd finally be happy. It has become a commodity, and the irony is that this type of 'organised happiness' – i.e., achieved through planning and goal-setting versus spontaneity – doesn't even feel like happiness by the time it arrives in your life.

The goal of happiness is a good and positive one – I would never want to deny someone that. But the exception is when your life isn't on the same trajectory as everyone else's. Then, it quickly rots and decays, and what should be a powerful motivator and generator of goodness then churns up all the anxiety and negativity within.

In any case, desperately trying to make happiness your permanent state can be disastrous.

After our Bay of Islands trip, I have a few weeks in Auckland before heading off again to the South Island. Sitting in a sunny reading nook in Felicity's house, I think about how the expectation to be happy is associated with certain points in your life. For instance, if you are married, you must be happy. If you have kids, you must be happy. It doesn't allow much room for confessing when things aren't going well. No wonder most people tuck away what's really going on behind 'I'm fine'.

A better navigator for life is meaning.

'I came across this piece from [the psychoanalyst] James Hollis,' Oliver Burkeman said when I emailed him about the book he wrote on happiness, 'which is that when facing any decision small or large, don't think about whether it will make you happy, because we are terrible at predicting that. Think about whether it will enlarge you or diminish you. That makes things a lot clearer.

'I can't tell whether something is going to make me happy, but I can tell when I am stepping up to the plate or whether I am hiding.'

Although I feel that making the decision to leave my job and go travelling was stepping up to the plate, I feel like I'm hiding. I'm living but it's not living if I'm too scared to take any step that means having a connection with someone.

There is so much going on in my head – kids, Rob, love, work – and I feel so untethered to everything I know.

I know meaning is the right star to set a course for, but I don't know what will give my life meaning. All I know right now is that I quit a good job to go travelling and I am moving further and further away from what my life used to be. The realisation sets a flutter of panic beneath my heart that refuses to dissipate.

I should know this by now – that anxiety starts slowly, and then picks up pace until it's moving so fast, it becomes a blur. But when it is creeping upon you, you can't look directly at its face and see that it is coming for you.

After about two weeks of this, a fortnight of feeling it cluster at the corners of my eyes, creep into my pillowcase and worm into my breath, I feel it growing heavier, and more serious. It's harder to get up in the morning. It sits inside me like my blood is turning to lead.

I know what I need to do – I need to tell someone. I need to phone a fucking friend. But I can't. Despite being surrounded by people – my in-laws, Rob's friends, my friends – despite knowing what I should do having written so many things about mental health, I can't. I don't know what has brought this on – I mean I quit my job, for fuck's sake! This is the least pressure I have ever been under. But not knowing only fuels the panic.

I definitely can't tell anyone at home about this because then it feels as if it will mean that I have failed doing New Zealand. That I brought this on myself by coming here despite the fact that the times when I have felt close to disappearing, when I have felt my most unbearable pain, was in London, surrounded by loved ones.

The problem with depression and anxiety is that depression robs you of your energy and anxiety churns your ability to speak into an incomprehensible mess. I don't have the energy to grab the words, and then, when I do, I am overwhelmed and surrounded by so many of them I don't know which ones to grab.

Why is this happening?

The obvious factor is that it must be to do with Rob. But I rack my brain – London is a far harder place to deal with Rob stuff because that's where we lived our life. There is virtually no part of the city that doesn't contain a fragment of a memory with his smile, the touch of his hand or his loping walk in the frame.

I don't know if it's Rob, an unravelling of myself, a feeling of being lost. I know that if 90 per cent of my brain is operating on an unconscious level, there are things happening that are murky and dark.

But when Felicity goes away for a long weekend to visit some friends, that's when the shit truly hits the fan.

~

I'm going to describe the location first.

Felicity's house is a cottage, and she spends a lot of time and effort on her garden. The front is the prettiest collection of trees, shrubs and flowers. There is one bush with tiny white flowers that bumblebees have claimed as their own, as I discover when I water it with a hose and disperse a lot of disgruntled insects.

Up the stairs and over the deck, and through the front door. To the left is the hobby room, where Felicity sews her beautiful dresses or paints. To the right is her bedroom, a pretty little suntrap where Finbar likes to hold court on her bed.

Down the corridor, the cottage widens and stretches into an open-plan kitchen and dining room on the left, and a living room on the right. The next annexe is the guest toilet and room (my little domain) and, beyond that, the back garden.

On the day it happens, I wake up late. I don't have to worry about whether anyone else will think I'm being lazy because there is no one in the house.

Normally on a sunny day, the light hits the front of the house first, and slowly works its way through, warming it up, until it hits my room in the afternoon, making it the perfect napping spot.

On this day, there is no sun. It's as if while I was sleeping, the sky peered into my mind and created something to reflect its contents. There is only rain, thick and heavy rain, the kind that will flood and drench your defences in minutes.

I wake up and wash my face. I look at my chewed-up toothbrush and make a note to buy a new one. I feel really sluggish, so I have a shower and close my eyes under the hot water, willing the sluggishness to seep out of me and trickle down the drain.

I wear comfortable clothes, ones that feel kind and soft on my skin. I put the kettle on to make tea and try to formulate a plan of what to do with my day, but the thought is slippery. I can't get traction on it and I think absently about what to have for breakfast.

While I wait for the kettle to boil, I sit in the living room and flick on the television. A programme comes on and then, when I hear the loud click of the kettle switching to off, I find I can't move.

I'm both hot and cold, and a dread slides down my spine and commandeers my arms, my legs. I knew, I *knew* it was here – why did I pretend I couldn't hear it or that I'd snap out of it?

I heard the wings of it beating before it arrived. It clung to the shadows in the corner of walls, it hid in whispers under the bed. It remained ever so cleverly out of sight yet at the same time present, the tip of its tail, the smell of its breath, reminding me it was there, and then again not.

When it arrives, it slinks out of the shadows. It is daylight. I am in a place, a home, I feel loved. But it comes anyway, and it bares its teeth and says:

You feel terrible.

You will always feel terrible.

You are going to die.

It repeats the last line over and over again.

I feel Rob's death around me; it is a quicksand around my feet. I'm not in England, I'm not at home. I am in New Zealand, and I don't know how to call for help. I am paralysed, I want this to be over with. I am going to die. Rob's death is finally going to kill me. This is what I have been terrified of. That, eventually, his death will catch up to me and claim me too.

What do I do? How do I stop feeling like this? What must I remember? Am I GOING TO DIE?

Remember, this is a panic attack. *Think, Poorna.* What happened the last time I had a panic attack as bad as this? I was with Rob, in Goa, and he held my hand and made me breathe properly. I put aside the sharpness of missing Rob and I breathe. Slowly feeling returns to my hands and I can move.

I decide I have to leave the house. I go to the gym, but the feeling still follows me. It's not a cute puppy nipping at my heels; it is a black oil slick that clings to my shoes, travelling up my spine and curling around my brain. I work out; I try to forget. Louise, a childhood friend of Rob's, now my friend, texts me out of the blue. Do I want to meet for coffee?

I half-type a reply that I'm busy but something hits override and says: 'Yes.' We meet for coffee. Louise thinks she is speaking to all of me, but she is only addressing 50 per cent. The other half has been shoved behind a curtain, like an unsightly mess when guests are round. She can't be allowed to see it, and it takes every ounce of energy to ignore its chittering, which I drown out with a mantra: Keep Your Shit Together. I tuck my thumbs tightly into my palm. It's a small gesture that no one will notice but it strangely soothes me or, at least, keeps me sane for the time I'm out in public.

I tell Louise before we part ways that I'm struggling a bit and I'm glad we met. She looks concerned, and asks how I am, but I still can't tell her everything that is going on with me.

She offers to drop me home, and we chat about other things. I look out the window as we drive past my favourite sushi shop in Takapuna, and we get stuck in traffic on Lake Road on the way home, chatting some more.

I can't say it to her in the car, and I don't know that I could ever say it to her because acknowledging the words, the feelings, makes me terrified for my existence.

But Louise probably saved my life, or, at least, my sanity, as it teetered on an abyss. I flicker between thoughts of life and death as we pass the fruit shop that Felicity loves visiting. I think absently of picking up some cherries which are ripe and in season. I am glad that I have started thinking of things like cherries.

I start silently naming fruit to keep this fleeting feeling of calm going: cherries, plums, peacherines, peaches, nectarines, apples, pears, feijoas, cherries, plums . . .

Although meeting Louise helped, when I get home, the feeling returns and now I know I am in trouble.

Whenever I have had a panic attack, it passes, and I feel exhausted but better. I began having them when Rob's problems started to get really bad, but then I didn't have them for a long time after that.

After Rob died, I have maybe had two of them. But they have always dissipated. This is the strongest and longest panic attack I have ever had.

Once I'm back in Felicity's cottage, I feel this unbelievably strong certainty that I am going to die. That if I do not get on a plane back to England RIGHT NOW I am going to die in this living room and that will be the end of me.

I don't know how, but I know with certainty it's going to happen.

Maybe I'll lose control and kill myself. I always knew

people bereaved by suicide are at a much higher risk of suicide themselves and, finally, it has come to make good on its promise. I mean I don't want to kill myself, but I am so convinced in this moment it's going to happen.

When I look back on this, it seems ridiculous, because of course I wasn't going to die in Felicity's sweet little cottage. But at the time, I was sure of it. There was nothing you could've said to convince me otherwise.

I decide I can't be in the living room. And I can't watch television because I can't focus on anything.

So I wait in my room. And I read.

I slow down my breathing and I face a wall, breathing in and out, in and out.

You're alive, you're alive, you're alive.

This will pass, this will pass, this will pass.

Somehow, I fall asleep. Somehow, I make it to the morning. The feeling returns but not in such intensity. It's like watching an old television and seeing the images flicker in and out between white noise.

In five days, I will be going to the remote west coast of the South Island for my solo road trip. There is a part of me that is terrified that I may end up in that dark place again and no one will be around to help me. But in the same breath, I feel relief at the prospect of being lost, because at least if I lose my mind no one will be around to see it. For all the work I have done around being honest in my life, there is still a huge part of me that doesn't want my loved ones to see me unravel. I want everyone to think I am handling this well, and I can't stand the thought that they might be worried about me.

Further down the line, it takes time and the right collection of words from a friend to articulate it, but this inability to let go, making out like I have my shit together all the time, keeping up appearances, is gasoline in the tank for the part of my brain that likes to people-please.

~

In the space between my panic attack and my trip to the South Island, life moves at a very slow, sludge-like pace. I meet Gabrielle for brunch and we talk about work and music and life. I go to the gym. I visit the cemetery. I don't cry again, not for a while.

Somehow, I inch my way to the day I need to leave for the South Island.

When I tell my friend Tania about this much, much later when I am back in England and we are in that sweet, lazy part of the afternoon after a lunch of food and white wine, she says, 'I don't know what caused it, but it seems obvious why you were able to get to that point where you could start the trip and be okay with being on your own.'

We had just been talking about my panic attack.

'Poo,' she said gently, 'you give a lot of yourself to people. You're always worrying about whether they are okay and what you can do for them. And a big part is that you're worrying about inconveniencing people or showing that you're struggling. So no wonder you felt better when you were on your own because even if things weren't awful, they certainly weren't great, but you didn't have to pretend to anyone that you were fine. When you weren't.'

It definitely explained why those feelings dissipated, but it didn't explain why I had the panic attack in the first place. That wouldn't come until later.

~

In Nelson airport, I start the car – a fat, sturdy red Kia with a four-wheel drive. The engine hums a little purr to say hello.

'Hello,' I say back. I check my mirror, touch my bottle of water reassuringly, check my sunglasses and hook up my iPhone to the sound system.

I'm still not sure this is a good idea, and not just because of I'm Going To Die day.

Two weeks ago, a storm battered the west coast and carved it up; the sea ate it like pieces of chocolate. Two days ago, there was a cyclone that had less impact but shuddered 150km winds through the top of the South Island and ran out of breath by the time it hit the Southern Alps.

I'm driving solo, on roads I am unfamiliar with, but there is no turning back. I don't want to be the person who cancelled their trip because they were too scared. Plus, I may not get the chance again: to lazily explore the coast in this way, and on my own.

The thought hidden behind that is: at some point, maybe I'll meet someone. If that happens, I won't be able to take myself off solo for weeks at a time. For instance, when Rob was alive, it wasn't that he wouldn't have let me do it alone, but more that I didn't want to. I loved sharing my experiences with him and having him along for the ride.

I had to see this trip alone as the love letter to myself.

As I begin driving, the signs of town life peel away like tiny bits of shell, faster and faster as I pick up speed. Soon, the signs for plums and avocados, the cafés, the big DIY stores and supermarkets recede in the background, and all I am left with is the open road.

The road cuts into single-lane highways. On either side are grasses that tip into valleys that run down and gather pace, hitching up their green skirts and leaping into mountains and rivers and waterfalls into the distance.

It is greener than I could've imagined and, after a time, I feel as if I am heading into the centre of something that is both a landscape and, yet, myself.

People told me about the wildness and remoteness of the west coast, and that's exactly what I need. I feel wild and remote inside, and have done for some years, and there is a part that yearns to see myself reflected in my surroundings.

After a few hours of driving and a pit stop to pick up groceries, I get to the outskirts of Karamea. Most people don't normally come to this part of the coast unless they are doing a walk called the Heaphy Track, because it requires you to drive an extra hour and a half out of your way, up and down winding roads.

Most people like to make things easy and start at

Westport, the highest point on the west coast you can get to without needing to backtrack.

I didn't want easy and, besides, something was calling me north.

After a time, I catch the first gleam of the ocean and I pull over the car. There is no one for miles in front or behind me. I pick my way across some debris caused by the storm a few weeks ago, and I face the most dramatic, thundering beach I have ever seen. It is huge and powerful; a creature of air and water humming back and forth for miles and miles.

Its song begins somewhere deep down, and by the time it reaches my feet it is playing through the very last notes. There is spray on her tongue, silver in her voice where the sun catches her.

I feel humbled. I feel lucky. There are lots of rocks and I build a little tower to say to Rob, *I came here and said your name.*

I get back in the car, put some music on while I watch the theatrics of the ocean. Green Day, Faith No More, Smashing Pumpkins. Type O Negative's 'Black No 1', a song literally about black hair dye. I used to listen to that song when I was fifteen, blasting it on my Walkman while taking the train to go and meet my friends.

I think about that girl, this beautiful, scrawny little thing with big green eyes, who wore leather boots and fishnet tights. I can almost recall in perfect clarity how it felt to lace up those boots, the eyeliner raccooned around my eyes.

How the only things important to her were a) good English grades and b) boys.

God, I miss her.

Or maybe what I miss is an existence where the most important thing that day was going to a record shop to buy a song about hair dye, and my biggest worry was whether a boy would notice me.

Who am I? I ask the seashells. *What manner of creature have I become? Will I forget how to love? What if I can never love again? What if all a man can see is my sadness and he's scared to love me?*

The ocean roars back but says nothing.

Later on, I arrive in the centre of Karamea, and there's a part of me that unfolds with the long stretch of road ahead. It is so quiet and empty. I feel a sense of relief that I have brought myself here.

That unconscious part of me knew I needed to be here, and I finally see why. I had to willingly take myself away, to choose this for myself. I wanted to get lost, and here I am, far, far away from anyone I know, everything I know.

The sense of peace carries upon those wild seas and pumps them down the long roads flanked in golden grasses.

After I park up, I meet Steve, the guy who runs the local motel, who also runs the local pub attached to it. As I walk in there are stares – not because I am Indian, but because I am a woman.

Seven guys are clumped around, looking shiftily into their beers, and something suggests they do this every day at 5pm.

The motel is strange – very clean, but like a perfectly

preserved 1970s suburban house. The shower is hot and there's a cooker so I can make myself some scrambled eggs with cheese. I fall into bed for a deep sleep.

The next day I head to Oparara Basin with my guide, an older lady named Yvonne. The basin is in a national park that sits at the top of Karamea, which is interwoven with a network of honeycomb caves.

After picking our way through the trees, we come across a basin filled with crystal-clear water stained the colour of syrup from all the tannins in the beech trees.

The remote location means the caves don't see a huge number of tourists, and it is part of the bedrock from back when New Zealand was part of the mysterious, now submerged continent of Zealandia.

Here is where the bones of extinct giant birds lie and living giant snails crawl. It is the closest thing I have heard of when it comes to magic. The ghosts of forgotten creatures whisper in forests of ferns and moss, the scent of their existence is so recent when compared to other parts of the world.

Yvonne tells me about her experience of living in Sydney. Her family is from a different part of the South Island, but she has lived in Karamea for some time because her ailing father is here. She loves the quiet of it. She can take her kayak out when the sea is calm, and her back garden is the bush filled with robins and fantails.

'I couldn't stay there for too long,' she says. 'I felt like the city was going to swallow me up.'

It makes me think about London. Most of the time,

when I worked in the heart of London and lived on its outskirts, I danced along to its same, frantic frequency. I would only notice the dissonance in moments when I stepped outside of it, or I was having difficulty keeping pace. Then, I felt as if it was going to swallow me up.

But being away from it, I don't think I feel like that about it any more. When I was in Nepal, I met a guy who is originally from the north of England, and we were talking about London, and the pressures to keep pace, and how people just drove themselves mad about the same two things: work and money. He has never lived in London.

He said, puzzled, 'But I don't get it. I would've thought that in a city, especially one like London, you have so much freedom to be whoever you want, do whatever you want.'

I sighed. 'You would think that, but people like to impose their own prisons wherever they go.'

At the time of that conversation, London and I were separated. I didn't want to go back to her. I was glad to be free of her. I resented how unhappy she had made me, how scared, tiny and cautious she made me feel about certain aspects of my own life.

Maybe it has been long enough, but when I hear Yvonne say that, I think no. I don't worry I will be swallowed up by London. I remember the London I first fell in love with while hanging out in my uncle's corner shop. It smelled sweet, it felt exciting, a bit grubby yet full of life, colour and fizz.

The purest result of travel is that it reminds you of how big the world is, how unfixed things can be.

A city can't gobble you up if your mindset is bigger than concrete and gasoline. You didn't just chance upon your life by accident – you built it that way. The reason travel is important is because it provides the backdrop with which to evaluate everything in your life.

Which is: you didn't happen upon your life, your loves, your friends, your work. You built it yourself. If you built it yourself, you can choose what to keep in it and what to remove. If you built it yourself, it means that even if the wrecking ball comes and smashes it to dust, you can build it again. How do you know this? Because you did it once before.

The following day, after Karamea, I drive to Punakaiki. Punakaiki was one of the places that had its road chewed up like a piece of tobacco and spat out into the sea by cyclone Femi.

On the way, I stop at the lookouts that mark the way to Punakaiki – it's evident the long, rolling sea is in a mood, thundering against the shoreline. The sky is the same colour of hurt: grey and full of sorrow.

I stop at a little track and watch the remains of sea plants spreading in a fan just out of reach of the water's fingertips. The sand is every shade of black and grey, tiny stones that flicker in the light.

Further down are the Pancake Rocks. I've gotten used to New Zealand's literal way of naming things: Hole in the

Rock, One Tree Hill, Greymouth, Cape Foulwind (smells of seal poop) etc. It's literally like someone said, 'What does that look/smell like? Oh, yeah, let's call it exactly that.'

Thank God for the Maori language and its beautiful complexity of meaning that overrides the blunt English names.

Hole in the Rock is Motu Kōkako, Greymouth is Mawhera. Even New Zealand, which was named by Dutch cartographers after a place in Holland called Zeeland, is Aotearoa, meaning 'the land of the long white cloud'.

The Pancake Rocks are pretty – layers of limestone shuffled on top of one another like a library of stone books, but there are too many people around. Backpackers incessantly discussing the topic of food or buses, old people who smell wonderful and clean, and young Instagrammers in incomprehensible outfits and carrying lacy parasols.

Afterwards, I hire a kayak near where I am staying to get away from them. Ken the kayak man informs me that the river is not swollen, but there are mini rapids.

'They are just small though and the others who went out this morning came back alive,' he says. Is Ken joking? I can't tell sometimes with the Kiwi sense of humour.

By the time I get to the river, I feel pretty silly for panicking. It's muddy where the rain has stirred up the silt, but in the middle it is shallow and crystal-clear. I dip into the water and head off into the bush. Rising up all around me are ferns, palms and birds flitting between the trees. Soon, it has swallowed me up in its quiet embrace. I can't hear anything – not the sea, the backpackers, nothing.

He wasn't joking about the rapids. They aren't big, but they require work, and my muscles take on that familiar, sweet rhythm of working through the water. I come across one particular gush of water and, no matter how hard I paddle, it won't let me through.

Then, I release my paddle and close my eyes as the current pushes me away. The silence has weight to it, but it is so beautiful and restful. I could sit in the moment for ever, but I know even a few seconds will stay with me in my memory, creating a place of stillness that I can visit over and over again.

The sensation is that of emotional weightlessness. I don't think I realised that the noise in my life wasn't just filled with the sound of other people's expectations. It was a discordant symphony of so many other pressures: each section was trying to play its own music but was deaf to what the overall harmony should be.

It was composed of what I expected from my own life, my sadness, my fear that I will never be okay so I have to wield powerful words to pretend I will be okay.

I am strong. I am capable. I am fine.

Just because I say a thing doesn't make it true, however much I want it to be. But that's a thought and emotion that isn't required right now. All I feel is the push and flow of water. I don't need to think. I don't need to say anything. It is peace at its purest because it requires nothing from me, and I do not require it to be anything. It just is.

Later on, I get settled into my hostel. 'You're in a *hostel*?!'

Priya texts. She and I are both princesses when it comes to travelling but arguably she is hardier than me since she goes to festivals and doesn't tend to leave after the first day like I do.

It came recommended and it's clean, and by the sea.

'Yes, but I'm not staying in a dorm,' I reply. Nepal has traumatised me against dorms somewhat – I am just too old and paranoid about my snoring/farting habits to share a room with strangers. Also everyone looks incredibly young, which makes me feel like a weirdo lurking around a school playground.

I see them scurry around with their houmous, bread and cheap wine, and they are having an amazing time, the first adventure of many.

Being around them reminds me of a date I went on a couple of months ago, when I was bored in Auckland and tinkering around with dating apps.

It was with a very handsome Belgian guy named Lucas who was travelling around as a photographer but also wanted to fulfil his lifelong ambition of playing . . . baseball.

I don't know whether language was a barrier, but when I tried to ask him questions about his life, he wouldn't go into any detail. Such as:

Me: So, baseball? That's pretty unusual for a Belgian guy, and to come to New Zealand to play?

Lucas: Yes, I like baseball and this seemed like a good place to come and play it.

Me: Really? Because, you know, New Zealand is usually known for its rugby?

Lucas: Is it?

He liked to have long pauses punctuating the conversation. Long pauses make me very twitchy, so I talk twice as fast to fill the gap. He looked at me like I was on cocaine. 'Are you okay?' he asked, which made me even more paranoid and made me talk even faster.

But then he opened up a bit about his life. He was a few years younger than me, but still in his thirties. He'd been travelling for two years, and his parents were concerned about him not coming back to Belgium.

Two years might make him sound like some kind of maverick, and, indeed, before planning my big trip, people said to me, 'Well, you might decide not to come back.'

But I don't really get the travelling indefinitely thing. I don't understand how, at some point, you don't want your loved ones near you, or at least your friends.

His idea was to play baseball with various small teams, and then he announced he was writing a book about happiness. But he couldn't articulate what would be in the book, and I stopped asking questions after he said, 'It's a challenge writing it without a laptop.'

I feel like Lucas's 'I'm writing a book on happiness' line possibly only works on women much younger than him who haven't written a book.

When I pushed him on his backpacker lifestyle, he said he stayed in hostels and then started describing how the one he was staying in at the moment was great because they did $3 meals.

I don't know if it's snobbery on my part, but the $3 meals story just made me want to get up and leave. I thought: here is a guy, in his thirties, who doesn't know what the fuck he is, or who he wants to be. He's writing a book on happiness but doesn't have a computer, he plays baseball in a country that is probably least known for its baseball, he's travelling indefinitely while claiming government benefits from Belgium – and he thinks it's freedom. Maybe it is freedom to him, but not to me.

It crystallises something I've been struggling with, which is: what is freedom? I'm talking about it from the privileged Western point of view, because obviously in some countries freedom is literally about basic human rights such as women being able to drive or not being bombed. But in our bubble, we have this notion of freedom that if only we weren't held down by our jobs/loved ones, we'd be free like wild horses and would gallop into the distance.

But we already know that the brain creates its own prisons (thanks, Srini), no matter how much freedom we may actually have. And I know, for instance, that money allows you freedom but it can also trap you into thinking it's never enough.

For Lucas, maybe it's important that he can roam around playing baseball. But if I was him, being able to afford $3 meals and living off dole money would not be my marker of a good life.

I start thinking about what a good life would be. For me, it would probably mean a job that didn't involve managing people. It would mean being somewhere remote and peaceful from time to time, and honouring that regularly. It would be working on the things I love doing but making money from it.

Money isn't everything, but it does give you options, I realise. The life of a nomad may seem alluring because it seems free of responsibility, but all you are doing is bringing your basic needs back down to a very primal and fundamental level, for instance needing to be fed.

There are plenty of people for whom that is not an option, and I wonder what it says about people who can shrug off their life of material privilege for a while and then come back to it as if they never left. I think about my own privilege. When I was in India talking to some friends, they were saying how hard it was to get a visa to Singapore. Singapore! A place I wouldn't have thought twice about hopping on a plane to visit.

Then I realised that my British passport meant I could go to so many places and not wonder or care about how tricky it was. Yet I was only granted that because my parents had made the decision to move to the UK, and it seemed completely unfair that people of the same race and family as me were faced with locked doors.

I wonder how that makes people feel – the ones who cannot move between the doorways of privilege so easily. Pissed off and unfair? My friends didn't seem pissed off, they just seemed ... resigned.

In order to escape the increasingly loud sound of

backpackers eating and discussing travel plans, I go and sit by the beach to watch the sun go down.

An hour before sunset, the sun comes out fully from behind the clouds, brokering peace between sea and sky. The waves arrive in long curls, starting off in a deep-green froth that transforms into pipes of bright-green glass shot through with beams of light as they hit the highest point they can go.

Just as quickly they dissolve into meek and mild white foam that disappears under the carpet of dark sand to begin the same journey.

I watch this scene over and over again. I press the corner of my mind like a tongue probing the tender spot of a wobbly tooth, but I can't find a whisper of those dark shadows that haunted me a couple of weeks ago. I am glad to be alive.

~

The next day, I head to Okarito. When I tell my New Zealand family and friends, most of them go, 'Huh?' I can understand why. It's so tiny, it's not on any of the bigger highway boards. It sits between Punakaiki and Franz Josef Glacier, and, of course, everyone wants to get to the impressive glacier, so they just whizz past.

The only reason I had heard of it was through a random search for kayaking in the area. I discovered Okarito, and read that it had a pretty lagoon.

Along the way, I stop at the most depressing town I've come across to date – Greymouth.

At first I think I'm being uncharitable – maybe it's the grey weather. A squall picks up just as I enter the town. Then I think, no.

The more places I pass through, whether it's for coffee, lunch or staying the night, the more I sense their personality and feeling. I'm not saying this emanates from the brick-work or concrete – I haven't totally lost it – but there is a very strong imprint made and left behind by people.

I first felt it when I went to Stone Town in Zanzibar with Rob. We visited the place where they once held slave auctions, and there was such an oppressiveness to it that I burst out crying. He put his arms around me, and I couldn't describe it other than a real sense of sadness, despair, so much misery stamped into those walls over and over again.

I imagine even if you don't know much about a place, you could still feel it. Greymouth is fucking sad. I don't know what happened here but it smells like a concentrate of broken dreams and hopelessness. There is a pretty, quaint railway sign, but it's not fooling anyone. I grab some para-cetamol and washing powder from the supermarket and zoom away as quickly as the Kia can go.

I stop at Hokitika on the way because the pictures I have seen of its gorge are incredible: milky, turquoise water that's a mix of rock flour and water. It is so beautiful and unearthly, inviting yet so cold – it's the kind of place you imagine holds the power to eternal youth. But the number of tourists is jarring; its real heart is hidden too deep for me to sense what it is actually like.

Finally, I end up in Okarito, and it's an antidote to the tourist masses of Punakaiki and Hokitika. There's a shonky little sign on the road indicating where it is, and the minute I arrive, I know I am in love with this place. I pop my head into the kayak shop, which has fresh carrot cake on the counter, and walk past a beautiful historical building called Donovan's Store (it's not actually a store).

Down the only main road, called The Strand, there are houses and a little statue that makes up the entire square. It has about thirty residents in total, and if you want to get food or petrol, you have to drive to Franz Josef.

Ahead, I hear the rumble of the Tasman Sea, and walk towards the shoreline to say hello.

Behind me rises a vast crop of foliage, the familiar fan of ferns cutting against the swollen sky. Houses perch above the hill in tiny little clumps. There is something special here, and it feels like a place I could live in despite there being nothing here that I'm used to. I've never lived in a place without a shop down the road or people about, but the frequency of this place hums to me, and I hum back.

The silence threads its fingers with the wind, but it isn't desolate or forgotten.

Further down the shoreline is a man fishing.

I wonder how he will cook what he catches. Grill it? Barbecue it? What kind of home does he live in? Is it warm and cosy? Or will it let in the wet, which threatens us with its presence with each passing minute?

At my feet, the rocks are all different colours, ranging

from the purest white to little Dalmatian rocks of black and white. Behind me, wheat-yellow sea grasses toss their hair across the black sand.

The sea is rough; I imagine here it is always rough as it hits the estuary. Would I be able to live here? I imagine the house I'd live in, the little car I'd buy to go and get groceries. Then I stop. Why do I always do this?

I imagine myself in a story, but I never imagine the hard parts. I think of the soft woolly jumper but never the relentless cold that requires it; the warmth of tea and biscuits but never the money earned to buy them. My whole life, I have told myself a narrative. If I marry the love of my life, I'll be happy. If I quit my job and leave my friends and family, I'll find peace because there won't be anyone to challenge me. If I don't have the stress of work, I'll finally understand myself better.

The fact is, that silence – true, beautiful silence – isn't just offering a respite from the noise of urban living. It offers peace, this much is true. A lack of connectivity to a cellphone network if you are lucky. But in the absence of noise, the price it exacts is that of a reflection bowl, and you cannot look away. There is no narrative you can tell yourself that can alter what you see staring back at you.

There is no story that I can tell myself about moving to Okarito that will fix or remove my sadness. There is no shortcut to honesty, no quick route to inner peace and resilience. Silence is soothing, but it is also utterly searing in what it forces you to confront, which is: who creates your loneliness? Who makes your choices? Who is responsible for your life?

I believed, with every inch of my heart, that I was in search of silence to figure out what I wanted from my life, free from the expectations of other people. But what I've realised is that silence is not just being in the mountains or out on a lagoon.

Unless I enter into a life of hermitude by buying a jumper, a kayak and moving to a remote shack, I am going to be in situations where that silence must be carried within me. Where I draw so much strength from it that I could be surrounded by a thousand people shouting what they think I should do and, in the midst of all of that, take a deep breath and know myself. Truly know myself.

I hadn't realised it, but this whole time I had been building a shell. Like a hermit crab, I had been adding bits of padding to it by not seriously thinking about what I wanted. It was easier to pretend like I didn't give a shit about love because then I wouldn't get hurt. It was easier to remove myself from my friends and family because I then didn't have to think about my future. It was easier to move to a part of London where I didn't know anybody and I could keep everyone at arm's length.

But eventually, what did that future look like? Would it be a life filled with love and mess and sweat where I could occasionally take off when I needed to be alone? Or was it going to be a life filled with the wrong kind of solitude, where the silence wasn't this nurturing, benign creature, but simply an emptiness, an absence of everything good?

In order to craft the silence into something good and powerful, I need to think about where I am going, what I want to do.

What I need is a list. It looks something like this:

- Sign up to a boxing match.
- Own a puppy and keep it alive and happy.
- Live near a river or lake so I can kayak.
- Go for one hike a year.
- Get a job that pays enough so I won't have to worry about money, but not too much that I get trapped by it.
- Think about adoption.
- Go on a date with my serious hat on.
- Figure out what made me think I was going to die (this almost didn't make the list).

I don't think that list includes upping sticks to one of the most remote parts of New Zealand.

~

Before I leave Okarito, I head out in a kayak on the lagoon. It's hard to imagine the lagoon occupies the same geography as the sea, still crashing into the shore as if demanding an answer to its wildness. Here, the water is still, like glass.

Ahead of me are wetland grasses, yellow fronds melting downwards into orange where they dip into water.

To my right is the treeline. Although you can hear the distant roar of the sea curled in the edge of your ear, there is none of that bluster here. I paddle away from the jetty and towards a small grove of trees. I'm transfixed: behind them, in the distance, are the Southern Alps, their tips capped in snow.

The water is so still, so mirror-like, that as I'm heading towards a curve in the lagoon, I cannot tell which is the land and Alps of my world, and which is the world that has just been unlocked in the water's reflection. If I angled my paddle in the right way, I feel as if I would drift into this alternate universe, where another Poorna waits, leading a different life.

The sensation of two worlds existing at the same time stays with me. Everywhere I turn and paddle, I see the same smudging of reality. I close my eyes and imagine this other existence. Is she happy? Did she go through the same heartbreak I did? Did she go through worse?

I drift off to a cluster of grasses at the edge of the lagoon, and just float in the water. I feel my mind reaching for that desperate, illogical place of trying to find Rob.

Every now and then, I entertain the maddest thoughts that maybe Rob didn't die.

Maybe he faked his own death and he's now happy and peaceful somewhere. Or maybe he did die and is now wait-ing for me in some parallel dimension, happy and peaceful somewhere. And if I just got to the same place as he was, and talked to him, and told him how much I loved him, how beloved and missed he was, that would somehow fix things.

But then it passes. The real world elbows its way in, whether it's through the flutter of spoonbills or the boom of the ocean. It dissolves the dream world; it cleanses me of illusion.

When I sit in the reality of my life, in a kayak, on the stillest water, with the elegant silhouette of a white heron in the distance, it shows how far I have come. I sought silence for respite from a life I wasn't sure I wanted to lead, but in turn, it has allowed me to confront the toughness in it. For the first time in a long time, I don't want to escape my life; I want to actually live it.

There are things I am sad about, that I will always hold an immense amount of grief around, but there is so much love in my life. I don't want to leave that behind or let it go.

I like my life: the safety and the risk-taking, the possibilities and the future-planning; the smallness of the world met with its vastness.

I like it all.

11

THE CICADA'S LAST SONG

When I return to Auckland, I begin winding down my days with everyone here. I spend time in bars by the waterfront, meet my friends David and Louise for lunch, go running along Narrow Neck beach.

I spend time in Orewa with Prue and David. We go for a long walk with Monty, who wants cuddles all the time and isn't fussy about who he gets them from. There is sunlight and tea by the time we return with specks of sea salt around our ankles.

I go on my friend Wesley's yacht and we drink beer in the sun while the Hauraki Gulf sloshes at our feet.

I see my friend Jools, whom I met two years ago while heavy in my grief on the Milford Track, and whose light-filled house I have found myself in at every available opportunity. She makes me coffee, I chat to her sister Margo who has also become my friend on this trip, and as we laugh, I marvel at the wonder and surprise of making new friends.

I buy one of my last ferry tickets from Devonport to the city and look as the sun catches the curve of the little sandbar by the dock.

This is home, this is home, this is home. I know everyone here is worried this may be the last time, but it's not. I came to see if there was more than Rob, and there was; there is.

I am left with the feeling of immense peace after the South Island, and I carry it within my heart like a secret.

I tell people about the experiences I had, I post pictures on Facebook of me standing in front of squashed rocks and eerily blue waters. But I'm not yet able to articulate the profound impact inside me.

After a few days in Auckland, whether it is because it has the familiar grind and buzz of a city, I feel that frisson of anxiety returning. I feel as if I should've had some definitive answers before getting on that plane back home.

I know that it will not do to get on a plane for twenty-four hours and have a panic attack. So I set up a Skype call with my therapist Isobel, to try to get some answers around why my big panic episode happened in the first place.

My expectations are low: not because Isobel isn't amazing at what she does, but because I have an Eeyorish outlook: maybe my brain has finally succumbed to madness. *Maybe this is who I am now.*

As we talk and I recount the panic attack, I have an epiphany. 'Oh, God, I know what it is,' I say.

Isobel says with infinite patience, 'Tell me what you're thinking about.'

I don't want to. Because that will make it real, and I don't have the energy for it. But it has emerged from the shadows and arrived in solid form, and there is no avoiding it.

When I was at the bottom of that metaphorical sea at the start of my grief, things were safe. Yes, I was in a state of extreme sadness, and yes, I probably thought about not existing about 70 per cent of the time. But I didn't have to worry about being hurt by anything else, because the hurt in my world was so huge, it eclipsed everything.

When I started making forays back into the world – whether it was dating or deciding to quit my job – yes, I was moving forward. But I wasn't really moving forward. All of those things were designed with a safety net in mind. I dated people I knew I wouldn't get close to. Quitting work was a big and brave decision (by my standards anyway), but it enabled me to escape the pressures I felt, rather than genuinely examine and work through them.

When Rob died, the big part of subterranean me said, 'We cannot ever be hurt again.' And so we went about crafting a life where we reduced the risk of that happening in every interaction, every scenario. But you cannot compartmentalise life like that. Even if you will your emotions into a state of order, there is always going to be the wild you that is not having any of it.

The panic attack was the price I paid for saying to myself, *We don't need love, we don't need kids and we'll be fine and safe and life will be okay.*

Just because things didn't work out with Rob, it did not

mean that I didn't want love in my life, or that I wanted to rule out having children. But I also felt like there was a massive block and that I wasn't capable of those things. Because by actively saying, 'I think I am ready to be in a relationship' or 'I think I want to have kids', I was opening myself up to variables I couldn't control: my happiness in the hands of another.

The feeling that flooded through me was dread.

'Okay,' Isobel says, and I already know what she's going to make me do, 'so where is that feeling in your body, and what does it feel like?'

I don't want to, I don't want to, I think. And another part of me: *Poorna, it's time.*

'It feels like it's in my torso, and it feels like cement,' I whisper. And I realise exactly what the block is, and I close my eyes against the reality of it.

Isobel squints at me through my screen. 'Tell me what's going on,' she says gently.

I take my time because this feeling is so vast. It has sat at the back of every thought, every action. Every article I have ever written about Rob's death, every romantic interaction with anyone, every time I've actively done something to make myself happy. It hasn't lurked or stalked me; it has been so closely fused to my bones, I didn't even notice it was there.

I made it a part of me the moment I got that phone call from Prue at one in the morning three years ago.

'I don't think,' I croak, and then clear my throat. 'I

have never, and I do not forgive myself for Rob's death. No matter the logic, I should have been there. If anyone should've been there, it should have been me. I should have saved him and I didn't. I should have known, and I didn't. I should've gotten on a fucking plane to see him before it happened, and I didn't.'

Isobel doesn't tell me that I shouldn't feel guilty. She doesn't say it will be alright. She doesn't say, 'It's not your fault' as every single one of my friends and family would have done in that moment. She doesn't say any of those things because she knows that she cannot be the person to offer me absolution.

Only one person can do that.

'I want to tell him so much that I'm sorry. I want to tell him I'm sorry I wasn't there, and I will never, ever be able to do that, Isobel, so I'm fucked. I don't deserve to be happy. I don't deserve to have another person fall in love with me because look at what happened to the last person I loved. He was mine to look after, and I failed him.'

I need Rob to tell me it is okay, and accept my apology, but that could never happen, which meant I would always push other men away and I wouldn't ever be able to let anyone come close to me. Basically, I'm doomed, hence the sense of dread.

Isobel makes me do silly shit from time to time, and this time, she makes me lie on the floor. 'Do you want to say sorry to Rob?' she asks – now just a disembodied voice coming from my phone.

I nod. Then I realise she can't see me. 'Yes,' I say half-heartedly.

I say I'm sorry. I say it over and over again and I'm crying, and the carpet feels damp from where the tears are trickling down the side of my face. But I realise the futility of it. I can say a thousand 'I'm sorrys' until the day I die, and I will never reach forgiveness. But that is because I am asking the wrong person for forgiveness. I tell Isobel this.

'Do you feel ready?' Isobel asks. I croak another yes.

I say my name in its entirety. Poorna means complete, and when I was a child, it was a running joke in my family that I was named that because I had all my fingers and toes.

But Poorna is the name given to the world by the god Brahma when he had finished creating everything. It is a name that invokes power. It appears in Sanskrit scripture over and over again to signify both the beginning, and an end.

My name is the umbrella under which our entire world sits. Long and lazy summers where love and lust and sleep intertwine, icy winters to freeze the hearts of little creatures, vast mountain ranges that line the earth's back, oceans holding a thousand fishy secrets. Death, love, life, birth, forgiveness, sorrow, sadness, shame, joy, hope. Things are born, they grow, and always, they die.

I say my name – this name – and I say, 'Poorna, I'm sorry. I am so sorry, I am so sorry. Forgive me, please forgive me.' By the end of it, I am crying so hard, the tears feel so hot, like they are bubbling from under the lid of a saucepan.

Afterwards I feel so empty – like a melon whose insides have been scooped out. I don't think I am 'fixed', and I don't think this is the end of it, but it's the start of a road to forgiveness, and that's something I didn't dream was possible.

When I get off the phone to her, I feel better than I have in months. I feel like, for the first time in a long time, there is a glimmer of a future. I wasn't ready to say goodbye to the idea of being loved, and trying to force that was causing this massive internal earthquake. Whoever, or whatever, my future may hold, slowly, ever so slowly, in the tight bud that is me, a petal unfurls.

I go for a very long walk, and I turn that moment of forgiveness over and over in my mind. I hold onto it very tightly, like a piece of gold I have found at the bottom of that dark internal ocean.

When I talk to her again a week later, I mention children and how I've started thinking about adoption.

'I think you have a lot of love to give,' she says. 'I think you are incredibly nurturing and good at relationships, and I think this other part of you is crying out for that to be fulfilled.'

The part of me that remains terrified is wondering how this will all work out.

But, I say to myself, you're asking a thing that hasn't been formed, that has no name. It either will, or it will not, but asking yourself if you're ready is still not the right question. Your heart is open, and there are parts of you that are ready, and parts of you that are not. And the parts that are not can only be answered and healed by him, whoever he is. And if you never meet him, that's okay too.

As for being on the same track as other people: no one is on the same track. We may unify and cluster around our sameness, but each person has a galaxy condensed in their own heads.

In this galaxy is a different, unique set of experiences and emotions, ranging from happiness to despair, sadness to joy, fulfilment to emptiness, loneliness to connectedness. We don't know how big these galaxies are, which planet of emotion they are orbiting. We have no way of knowing if people are truly okay or are just pretending.

From the grains of golden sand in Karnataka to the crystal-clear waters of the Bay of Islands, from the pigeon-shit-spattered streets of London to the quiet snowy mountains of Nepal, each and every place has been daubed in the sadness and happiness of human hearts.

Although I realise I was on a physical journey to kick-start an internal journey, perhaps the reason I don't feel like I have a neat stack of answers is because this isn't the end of it.

The next year will bring change, and the year after that. All I can do is be guided by what I think feels right for me, and bend and flow towards that, knowing that my capacity for change is what strengthens me.

Perhaps it's not the answer I wanted in the here and now, but it's the answer that will prepare me for whatever there is to come.

I finish my trip with what I think I always knew, which

IN SEARCH OF SILENCE

is that we are incredibly rich and complex creatures, and when we release the bitterness of what should have been, and replace it with the broadest sense of love, we're able to move on.

~

My time in New Zealand started with the sound of cicadas, and as is fitting before I am due to leave, the air is silent. Their time is over too, for now.

I go to Rob's grave to say goodbye, to feel him there, but all I feel, when I look at the gravestone, is absence.

I walk to the bench nearby and look out over the estuary. I check my phone to see messages from Mum and Mal. Very soon, I am going to see my sister and let my niece cuddle me like a starfish while we watch *Trolls*. All these loves and more are carried with me every day. They have always been here. I have space in my heart for more, whoever or whatever that might be.

I look up at the sky. I feel the scattered particles of him somewhere out there, in the crest of a wave, in the breeze catching the underside of a bird's wing sending it soaring upwards.

He is out there growing into something else, moving and surging with the world's renewal. I feel the join of earth, sky and air, and I press my lips to where they meet, sending my love out to him.

I've survived the world, I think, but I've been scared by it. I pushed people away because I thought I couldn't handle any more loss. I was so sure that if I could prove I was fine being away from them, it would validate my need for self-protection. But the silence didn't indulge or lie to me, because it wasn't the right thing for me to do. It didn't let me pull away from the world because that isn't what living is.

I hold within me, still, the fire that made me choose a life with Rob despite all of the mess that came with it. It is not satisfied flickering as a sedate little tealight. When I'm ready, it wants to burn and illuminate my world like a bonfire. I just have to not be so afraid.

I feel that love come back like a sonic boom. It doesn't yet have words; it only has thought.

For a few moments, I sit in the silence left behind by the cicadas. It's the sound of time waiting, watching, passing, growing. I close my eyes against the sun and hold myself still and calm in the tiny pleasure of it.

You survived me, the thought finally says, *so you can survive anything. Now go out there, and be happy.*

Acknowledgements

Mum and Dad, how do I say thank you for being there, for loving me not just when I am easy to love, but also when I am a prickly cactus? For believing I can do anything? For providing me with a place at home that is always mine, for always making me feel safe and loved? I love you to infinity and beyond. Priya, my funny, fierce, ridiculously clever sister, we have watched each other grow up in the most difficult times, yet we are still those protective kids who use their own weird little language, lurk outside the loo door, and make each other laugh until we cry.

My beloved Bell-Lynch clan. Prue and David, my other mum and dad. My brothers John and Alan. We met through Rob, and now we have chosen each other. It is a bond for life. Thank you for your endless waterfall of love, your wit, intellect and warmth. (And Monty.) Felicity, thank you for giving me your home to write in and your love and generosity, and for joining me in India on the maddest of capers. Gabrielle, for your cheerleading and mutual cackling and your heart, which is as big and as open as the New Zealand sky we stood under.

To my Shetty family, thank you. You clever, beautiful people. To my stupendous grandparents whose courage and bravery warms the darkest parts of my heart.

For my wonderful Mal, who remains one of the biggest loves of my life. For my incredible friends and family who have all supported me along this journey: Hasiba, Poonam, Niaz, Martin, Tania, Karen, Rashme, Aarti, Yumi, Sonia, Alice, Ahmed, Pavi, Shweta, Wesley, Jesse, George D, Louise, David M, Kumaran, Gun, Jools, Paul, Margo, Mel.

Thank you as always to my team at Furniss Lawton and Simon & Schuster – Rowan, Rachel, Nicki, Fritha and Melissa.

And to the beautiful, wonderful legion of people who I have met online, whose messages and words have created this little community for me, just thank you for your endless support and kindness.